LIFE, LOVE, &
OTHER MYSTERIES

LIFE, LOVE, & OTHER MYSTERIES

ADVICE AND INSPIRATION FROM AMERICA'S #1 CHRISTIAN POP GROUP

BY

POINT OF GRACE

Denise Jones, Terry Jones,
Heather Floyd, and Shelley Phillips
with
Davin Seay

POCKET BOOKS
New York London Toronto Sydney Tokyo Singapore

POCKET BOOKS, a division of Simon & Schuster Inc.
1230 Avenue of the Americas, New York, NY 10020

ISBN: 0-671-56251-7

First Pocket Books hardcover printing October 1996

10 9 8 7 6 5 4 3 2 1

POCKET and colophon are registered trademarks of Simon & Schuster Inc.

Printed in the U.S.A.

This book is dedicated to our sisters Angie, Christie, Dayna, Donita, Katie, Misti, and Robyn. We love you for who you are and for what you've taught us.

Davin Seay would like to dedicate his work to Jordan Savanna Seay—his own little Point Of Grace.

Acknowledgments

When we first met with Sue Carswell, senior editor at Pocket Books, a year and a half ago, the idea of actually writing a book about Point Of Grace didn't just seem remote . . . it seemed impossible!

Now that the impossibility has become a reality, there are so many people that we want to thank for their guidance, support, and encouragement, not just in bringing this book to life, but also for making our lives so rich, so fulfilling, and so much fun. Among the many:

Our parents—Travis and Brenda Floyd, Jim and Bonnie Lang, Don and Janice Masters, and Joe and Sharon Phillips.

Our precious husbands, Stu and Chris, and husband-to-be David.

Our manager, Mike Atkins, and our dear friends Steve Seelig and John Mays.

Also, the wonderful people at Word Records, Atkins, Muse & Associates, the William Morris Agency, Ouachita Baptist University, and the Pocket Books team, including Publisher Gina Centrello, Associate Publisher Kara Welsh, Editorial Director Emily Bestler, and Craig Hillman.

A very special thanks to Davin Seay for hours of listening and putting our lives into words.

CONTENTS

PREFACE

A book?

About us?

That was pretty much our reaction when we first considered putting the story of Point Of Grace into words.

After all, we're singers, and anything we really want to say, we get across in our music.

But once we started thinking about it, we realized that there are some things, even for four singers, that can't be said in three verses, two choruses, and a slow fade.

"Such as?" you might be asking. Well, if you travel as much as we do, and meet as many people as we meet, you begin to realize that everyone has a story to tell, and more often than not, those stories can be fascinating, fun, and full of insight.

Our story is no different. When we think about who we are, where we come from, and how we formed this group, it sometimes sounds to us like a combination soap opera and fairy tale.

There have been so many chance encounters, near misses, and twists of fate that had to happen to bring us—and keep us—together, that even a Hollywood screenwriter would have a hard time dreaming it all up.

When we looked at it that way, the saga of Point Of Grace really was like an adventure story, one that brings together four separate lives and sets them out on a road of discovery.

But more than just a true-life adventure, our story is also about finding meaning, purpose, and fulfillment in everyday circumstances: it's about finding answers and searching for the truth; clinging to hope, working hard, and building our faith. It's about how God has worked through the joys and sorrows of our lives to perfect the plan He had laid out for us from the very beginning. Sorry, but we can't help getting a little carried away when we think about how it's all come together, and we hope some of our enthusiasm and gratitude comes through when you read our story.

We also hope it will help you to see the adventure of your own life and the way that God's plan for you is being fulfilled every day in every way. And, for those of you who really aren't sure who God is or if He can be a part of your life, we hope this book will help you to make that decision and to see that even with today's confusing choices there is still a way to tell right from wrong.

That's why, for us, sharing has always been so important. It helps connect us, one to the other. Maybe you'll see yourself in our story, and if you do, then maybe we'll have passed on some of the lessons and the blessing, the wisdom and the warnings, that we've picked up along the way.

That looks like a lot to accomplish, when you write it down in black and white. But please don't get the wrong idea: we're not trying to preach a sermon or give a lecture on the meaning of life. After all, we're just four average American women, and no matter how good-looking, talented, and intelligent (did we mention humble?) we may be, we're just as interested in having fun, being hip, and keeping up on events as anyone else.

Let's be honest: being in Point Of Grace, standing up onstage under a bright spotlight, having fans write us letters and seeing our picture in a magazine . . . that's great! We have a really good time together, with lots of laughs and general craziness, but there are also some serious issues that we touch on.

If you had a chance to hang out with us, log some miles on the tour bus, or kick back offstage after a show, we think you'd be surprised just how normal we really are. We like makeup and nice clothes, we read books and listen to CD's, and even try to keep up with our favorite TV shows. We spend a lot of time missing our husbands and boyfriends and a lot more time on the phone talking to them in between shows. We've all got our annoying little habits and strange quirks and mannerisms, and we all try to overlook each other's glaring imperfections (no easy task, we can tell you!).

Most of all though, we try not to take ourselves too seriously. That's pretty easy to do, when people around you start acting like you're something special. We're lucky we've got each other to remind ourselves not to get carried away, and if that doesn't work, the road crew is always on hand to cut us down to size and remind us that maybe we're not such a big deal after all.

When it comes right down to it, what we want to get across—in our music, in this book, and face-to-face—is who we really are, and not just some glossy image manufactured to dazzle, distract, or dumbfound you. With us, what you see is definitely what you get, and we're proud of that fact. That's why, in this book, we'll try to show you, as much as possible, the inside of our lives.

Like everyone else, we've had problems and doubts and failures in our lives, and like everyone else, God has used those hard places to better mold and shape us into who He wants us to be. We'd be less than honest if we didn't open up that part of this story to you, too.

Sure, we each have a long way to go toward being, like they say in the army, "all that you can be." But, we've also come a long way and each step of that journey, good and bad, is worth the telling.

If you've picked up this book because you like our music, you need to know that what we sing about comes directly from what we've experienced. We may not write all our songs, but the ones that we pick have special meaning to us and that meaning is, more often than not, an echo of something we've gone through, as a group or individually. Because we want to be real, we want you to know what those experiences have been. It might help you to better appreciate who we are. Or, it might help you to better appreciate who you are. We hope so.

But maybe you're reading right now for another reason. Maybe the only thing you really know about us is that we're Christians, or that we talk about sexual purity and other issues that are so important to kids today. Maybe you've picked up on some of the controversy that comes about because of the positions we take and the message we try to get across. Then again, maybe what you're really interested in is not so much who we are as what we stand for.

Naturally we get a lot of mail from people who either find themselves in some of the situations we talk about or are just curious about the stand we take. Along with all those letters, we also have the privilege of meeting and talking with lots of you after our concerts. You'd be surprised how often we hear the same questions and concerns, and not just about sex, dating, and marriage. We don't know what it is about people like us who are in the public eye, but it seems that we're expected to know the answers to a lot of life's biggest mysteries.

We don't, of course, but that doesn't mean that we don't have our own opinions. Sure, we can't solve everyone's problems, but when we put our heads together and try to think through some of the issues that are brought before us, sometimes we find that we've actually got something helpful, perhaps useful, to say.

So, when we started considering what we wanted to include in this book, we naturally went back to those questions that come up over and over again from all of you. We've included a list of them and added our own answers, insights, and observations about such things as self-esteem, finding a career, getting along with parents, finding your own identity in the crowd, God and religion, and, of course, saving sex for marriage. It's as close as we can get to actually having a one-on-one conversation with all of you.

Finally, when we thought about what a Point Of Grace book should really be about, we realized that as much as this is a story about "us," it's also a story about "me." Point Of Grace is made up of four distinct individuals, and behind the "we" we're talking about are separate people named Denise, Terry, Heather, and Shelley. It's our unique stories that make up this book, just as our lives have come together to create the music and ministry of Point Of Grace.

When you hear us in concert, on a record, or on the radio, you're hearing four voices blending as one. Take away any part and it just wouldn't be the same. Now, we'd like you to meet all the parts that make the blend and get to know us, up close and personal.

Denise, Terry, Heather, and Shelley
Nashville, Tennessee, 1996

MEET DENISE JONES

Name: Denise Radon Masters-Jones
Birthday: March 22, 1969
Birthplace: Norman, Oklahoma
Education: Three credit hours away from a Bachelor of Music Education, Ouachita Baptist University
Favorite Color: Blue
Favorite Food: Barbecue brisket
Favorite Clothing Designer: A Line, Anne Klein
Favorite Book: *Where the Red Fern Grows* by Wilson Rawls
Favorite Scripture: John 16:33
Favorite Actors: Tom Cruise, Meg Ryan
Favorite Vocalist: Sandi Patty
Favorite Musical Style: Country
Favorite Movie: *White Christmas*
Favorite TV Show: *ER*
Favorite Cosmetics: MAC makeup
Favorite Perfume: Perry Ellis 360
Favorite Holiday: Christmas
Favorite Animal: My dogs, Free throw and Alleyoop

Favorite Waste of Time: Walking around the grocery store or mall

Most Memorable Experience: Saying good-bye to my parents as they left me on my own for the first time at college

Most Embarrassing Experience: In a basketball game in the ninth grade against our arch rival, I had a chance to shoot a free throw with no time left on the clock. I air balled my shot and we lost by one point.

Happiest Memory: My wedding day

Saddest Memory: My grandmother's death

Most Treasured Possession: My relationship with God and my family

Best Personal Quality: Sincere compassion for others

Worst Personal Quality: Being too hard on myself

Proudest Accomplishment: Singing with Point Of Grace

Greatest Ambition: To be a godly wife and mother

Guilty Pleasure: Eating everything I see on the bus after a show

Highest Ideal: To know God so well that in every decision, action, and attitude my response will reflect Him

Standing onstage under a brilliant spotlight; looking out over a sea of eager, anticipating faces; hearing the first notes of the music swell and stepping up to the microphone—it's a thrill that never gets old.

Being in Point Of Grace has been both the adventure of a lifetime and a learning experience that's taught us all some very valuable lessons. The satisfaction that comes from reaching for your very best; the responsibility that's so much a part of being in the public eye; the challenge of making music that makes a difference in people's lives; and the strength of true friendship that has carried us through good times and bad—I wouldn't trade it for the world.

But I think one of the most important lessons I've learned over the years is the value of being myself— just who I am, as honest and up-front as I can be. Anybody who entertains for a living will tell you that appearances count: how you look and act, what you say and how you say it . . . it can all add up to either a short ride to oblivion or a long and fruitful career.

And, so often, appearances can be deceptive. What you might see under the spotlight—the smiling, gracious, and charismatic artist—could very well be a whole different person once the curtain closes—insecure, unfulfilled, or just plain unhappy. The distance between the excitement of center stage and the loneliness of a hotel room—between a public image and a private life—can often be as wide as the Grand Canyon—and just as empty.

But it isn't only performers and artists who can sometimes get caught between that illusion of what people see and the reality of that face in the mirror. I think we all struggle with appearances, with wanting to make the right impression on the world, even if it means hiding parts of ourselves that aren't so appealing, or concealing feelings that we'd rather not admit we have. Sometimes our deepest secrets are the ones we keep from ourselves, and the image we try so hard to guard hides a truth that's hard to face.

For me, that image has always been one of a perky, vivacious, and energetic go-getter, which really is a big part of who I am. I love people, having fun, and getting things done. Ask anyone who's spent any time with me—my family, my friends, the other girls in the group—and chances are they'll all paint the same picture—bouncy, bubbly, and brimming with vitality. Hyper? High-strung? I've heard those descriptions more than once in my life.

But as much a part of Denise Jones as all that might be, there's another side, too, another half of the whole me. That's a side that not too many people see, an aspect of who I am that I've kept to myself, protected and put aside for those moments when I can let down the appearances and express other feelings.

What are those feelings? Well, I wouldn't be totally truthful if I didn't say that they sometimes bring tears and fears, moments of feeling helpless or hopeless or just plain overwhelmed. Learning to accept those feelings, to let them out and let them be, hasn't always been easy.

I've struggled with keeping up appearances, with not admitting to myself or others that being a happy, high-spirited dynamo is only one half of a complete person. I've struggled with turning over control of my life to

God, with admitting that I can't always be in charge of everything, with understanding that feeling sad is just as important as feeling glad, and, finally, that being real means being honest and that being honest means realizing you're not perfect.

It's a lesson that comes from a lifetime of learning—a lesson I'm still trying to get right, day by day, and sometimes moment by moment. Fortunately, I've had a faithful God, a loving family, and some very loyal friends to help along my way.

Norman, Oklahoma, where I was born, may not be your typical midwestern small town, but it's as close as you're likely to find these days. There was a real sense of community there, a family connection that I'm sure I must have felt from the moment they handed me over to my mom in the Norman Municipal Hospital, March 22, 1969.

Of course, in my case, that family bond was more than just a feeling. Growing up, it seemed to me that I was related to practically everyone in town. There were my sisters, of course, Donita and Dayna, seven and five years older, respectively, which made me the baby of the family. Then my grandparents, with one set living just down the street and the other close by. My mom's brother was part of the family circle, too, along with his three boys, pretty much the same ages as we three girls. My dad's two brothers, with their five children, completed the picture. It seemed like, in that part of Oklahoma, Masterses (which was my maiden name) and Prices were as common as fence posts.

Because I was born into a strong Christian family,

my earliest memories are mostly set in church. I can remember waiting in the crib in the Sunday school nursery while my parents sang in the choir. Later, I recall singing as a family in church and learning how to harmonize in a trio with my sisters. I guess you could say that my whole childhood was set to music.

Faith in God was at the foundation of the Masters clan. My sisters would both go on to marry music ministers, and my dad's father had also been a preacher. It was in my grandad's church that I sang my very first solo, "Somebody Touched Me," at the age of three.

When I think of my dad back then, what comes to mind is a very quiet, shy, and gentle man—a man I loved very much. He and his brother ran the family business, a moving company, and while I don't think we ever had a lot of money, I never remember feeling that we were poor or didn't have as much as our friends and neighbors.

He also loved his girls, there was never any doubt about that. Even now, when he comes to one of our concerts, at least one button pops off his shirt from pure pride. My mom and I have always had a great relationship, but I would have to say that I was a real daddy's girl—and his favorite caddy.

He has always been a good provider and a loving man, even during the difficult times when he was really searching to find his place in life. I think it came as a reaction to his family being very involved, in both the town and our church. His own father had served a term as town mayor, and for my dad there were questions as to where he fit and whether he really believed everything that had been passed on to him, or whether he was simply expected to follow along because his father was such an influential man. There was a period of real adjustment for him as a young father, working six days a week trying to build a future for his family, and sometimes he'd ask himself if it was all worth it. The answer to that question came over time, as he was gently shown that true contentment can only be found in God. With that realization, my dad was finally sure of who he was and what he believed.

I got only one spanking from my dad growing up, and I can still see the pained look in his eyes when he turned me over his knee. I really do think it hurt him more than it did me. I'd stolen a piece of gum from Dayna, and since she was the kind of person who kept track of everything, it wasn't long before she reported my gum abduction to my mom. What got me into the most trouble wasn't taking that stick of gum, but lying to her about the deed. When I heard my dad coming down the hall after work I knew I was in for it: we were taught early on that the only thing worse than being up to no good was denying it afterward.

Since my dad worked most of the time, it was my mom who was the real disciplinarian in the home. She also had a job, running a day care out of the house, where she took care of the local teachers' children. But there was never a time I can remember when she didn't set aside whatever she was doing to make sure we girls were getting the mothering we needed.

Hands down, my mom is the best friend I've ever had. She's been there not just as a parent but also as a teacher, an encourager, and someone who always put me and our family before her own wants and needs. I guess most people feel that way about their mother, but for me, her influence and example were what shaped and molded me as I grew up. My dad was always available to play ball with me—we were both really into sports, including baseball, basketball, and golf—but it's my mom who I remember on her knees, praying for each of us, asking God to protect and guide us.

I think God answered her prayers by putting her right in the middle of our young lives. She sacrificed herself for her family, showing us a consistency and commitment that would set a standard for our own behavior.

Not that I always met that standard. As I grew out of my childhood and into my early teen years, it seems as though my mom was standing square in the way of everything I wanted to do. Of course, it's a time when every kid is going through changes they can't quite understand, but I think it really hurt my mom when I started pulling away from her, because we had always been so close.

I wouldn't call myself a rebellious kid, but I know I had an attitude problem, because my mom took the opportunity to point it out whenever I started acting up. Whatever it was that she wouldn't let me do or was forcing me to do, I would just sit there, staring off into space with my jaw set, trying to ignore her. I could be so stubborn, and then when she was finished giving me a piece of her mind, I'd rush off to my room and scrawl "I hate my mother!" across a page of my diary.

Just like when you think that the world revolves around your mother when you're little, I guess it's also normal, when you're a teenager, to think she's just there to make your life miserable. And maybe I would have gone on to the next stage as well—leaving home and living my own life before I came around full circle to realizing how much she meant to me. But God had other plans, and when He intervened, it was, in no uncertain terms, a wake-up call that gave me the chance to get a fresh start with my mom, even before I broke away completely.

That part of my story really began when I was six years old, when I first started asking questions about things I was being taught in Sunday school, namely God, the Bible, and especially the man they called Jesus. My dad took me to see the pastor, and he asked me a lot of questions about what I believed and why I believed it, and I guess I must have given the right answers because we prayed a prayer and the next Sunday I was invited to walk down the aisle and announce to the church that I'd been saved.

You may wonder if a little girl of six could really know exactly what she was saying when she asks Jesus into her heart. To be honest, I can't really answer that. I do know that I was scared. It was a big deal for me to take that long trip down that gray carpet with everyone watching and then have the pastor lean down and shake my hand just like I was all grown up. But I also remember the feeling I had of somehow belonging, of being safer and secure in the knowledge that, whatever it meant, I had been saved and that God loved me.

As time went on, that feeling never exactly went away. But it didn't get any stronger either. I think my mom and dad were happy that I had made a commitment to Christ at such an early age. If they had any questions about whether I was old enough to make such a decision, they kept it to themselves. I continued going to services, became an active part of our youth group, and was a part of all the church activities that were so important to our family and our community.

At the same time, because of what I was going through with my mom, as well as all the regular turmoil of those early teen years, questions kept growing in the back of my mind: was I really a Christian? If believing in Jesus meant being good, why was I always feuding with my mother? How could I act that way and still expect God to love me?

The questions became more urgent and pressing, until I was brought face-to-face with my doubts. It happened one weekend at a big revival held by the church. At the evening meeting the visiting preacher said something that cut me like a knife: "If you were to die tonight," he asked, "where would you wake up tomorrow?"

I started thinking about that over the next few months, wondering if I really knew the answer. That need to know for sure returned again at another youth event when they showed a movie about the end of the world. It was all about how, one day, Jesus would return and all the true believers would be caught up in the air and taken with Him to heaven. It really scared me, and as I left the church, I began to wonder if I really knew God at all.

Not too long after that I got home from school one day and walked into the kitchen, the screen door slamming behind me, the sound echoing through the empty house. "Mom?" I called. No answer. "Mom!" I shouted, but there was still no reply. I was completely alone in the empty house. "Oh my gosh," came the sudden thought. "Jesus has come back, taken Mom, and left me here!" I was terrified and my eyes started to well up with tears when I heard a familiar voice call out from the hallway. It was Mom, back from a visit to the next-door neighbor.

All of these incidents were heading toward an inevitable conclusion, one that finally came at a youth camp in Falls Creek, Oklahoma. I had confided my doubts and questions to a counselor who told me that what I needed more than anything was to get one-on-one with God, talk to Him directly, and tell Him what I was feeling in my heart.

I took that advice and found that when I talked to God honestly and up-front, I got a whole new sense of His reality. "Okay," I said. "I'm going to try my best to make you Lord of my life! I want to be used by you, but I need your help to realize what's right and wrong and to respond in a way that is pleasing to you. I'm not perfect, Lord. But I'm going to try my best!"

I think it was maybe the first time I had a real understanding of my limitations and God's provision. But it certainly wouldn't be the last.

The funny thing was, as I found out later, that my

mom had gone through a similar spiritual awakening that same week. The result was that we both made a real effort to reestablish our relationship and to get along together. While I'm sure I've had a few slip-ups along the way, that evening really marked a turning point in both our lives.

You couldn't say that I really hated school, but on the other hand, you couldn't say that I really loved it either. While I never got anything lower than a *B*, I always considered school something you had to go through, for reasons that were never made exactly clear to me. Of all the subjects I took, I think I liked math the best, and that was only because it was straightforward: if you knew how to solve the problem, you could get an answer and then move on.

But if studying didn't get me excited, I more than made up for it with my enthusiasm for extracurricular activities. I've already mentioned how I used to play all kinds of ball with my dad, but that was only the beginning of my interest in sports. By the time I was in junior high I was a certified basketball fanatic, spending hours shooting hoops in the driveway until it became dark and my dad would turn on the light over the garage so I could see where I was aiming. I loved basketball: the speed, the skill, the sheer thrill of racing down the court on a fast break or scoring a three-pointer right over the heads of the defense. It was a game that seemed to match my high-strung temperament, pushing me to the limits and giving me a way to channel some of that restless energy.

Basketball was also a great way to learn about teamwork, and a team was a great place for me to belong. Some of my happiest memories are of those hours spent practicing on the court, bumping and butting and jostling for a clear shot or jumping as high as I could for the rebound (which wasn't all that high, by the way).

But basketball was also a place where I learned some of life's harder lessons. My first coach was a wonderful instructor, a guy who really inspired us and gave us all an inkling of just how much fun the challenge of competition could really be.

But everything would change in junior high school when a new coach was hired. She seemed nice enough at first, but it didn't take long for us to realize that those exhilarating early days were gone for good.

What had before been an atmosphere of encouragement and mutual support suddenly became one of subtle pressures, discouragement, and emotional abuse. Those early years of adolescence are difficult at the best of times, but with her sometimes harsh and callous manner, that coach did a lot to undermine our team's fragile self-esteem.

At thirteen I was scrawny, gawky, a little bit of a thing, already convinced that I was ugly and uncoordinated, an impression that wasn't helped by the nickname I'd picked up along the way: "Spazz." Even though I had the security of family and friends, the coach seemed to tap into a part of me that felt awkward and uneasy. I've always been very hard on myself: I'm my own worst critic, and it sometimes seems that I'm never going to be good enough at whatever I'm trying to do.

Those feelings found their focus in basketball. It wasn't as if Dad, who was a great player in his own right, was putting the pressure on. It wasn't even the friendly family competition with my cousins, two of whom, Mark and Brent Price, now play professionally for the Washington Bullets. It was just something in me that fiercely wanted to succeed at the game, and when the inevitable losses came, I took them as much to heart as if they said something about my failures as a person.

What had to have been the most traumatic event of my teenage years happened when I was in the ninth grade. We were playing a crucial game with our arch rivals, Central Mid High, and for the first half, we were mopping up the court with them and racked up a twenty-point lead.

Then, for reasons I'll never figure out, the coach took out the starters and put in some of the more inexperienced players. Our lead dwindled to one before she finally decided to put the starters back in, and by that time we'd been sitting on the bench for twenty minutes and were as cold as ice. With practically no time left on the clock there was a foul called on one of the guards, which gave us a free throw. I was picked to make the shot. Well, you could have heard a pin drop as I stepped up to the free throw line. The basket seemed to be a million miles away, and even as I held my breath and released the shot, I knew I wasn't going to make it.

It was an air ball, missing the backboard by a mile and leaving me with a sick feeling in the pit of my stomach. I could hardly stand to go back to school the next morning and have to walk down that hall, where every eye seemed turned on me with a pitiless stare of condemnation.

After that, basketball just never seemed as much fun, and although I hung in there for the sake of the team and my own pride, I really began to lose focus on my own self-worth. God says that each of us is precious in his eyes, but during those difficult years I often wanted to hide even from him. It was a dilemma made all the more difficult by the fact that everyone knew me as the happy, gung-ho Denise and I felt like it was my responsibility to keep up that image, no matter how I felt.

The only person who really knew what I was going through was my mom, and I remember so clearly crying in her arms and asking, between sobs, "Am I crazy? Am I losing it? Because I just don't know who I am, anymore. . . ."

Looking back on those years, as difficult as some of them were, I can still see God's hand gently guiding me along. I got really involved in church life, especially my youth group. Considering how I sometimes felt about myself, I was so grateful to be surrounded by a bunch of kids who didn't put pressure on me to be cool or act out my feelings in rebellion. I think it might have been easy to stray during those rocky times, to say to myself and God, "I just don't care anymore. It hurts too much to try." But He provided me with a way out of myself and my problems. I also got a lot of wise counsel from a very caring youth minister. Drugs, alcohol, and sex were just not an option, no matter how much I felt that sometimes life just wasn't making sense.

And in a lot of ways, though, it did make sense. For all the confusion and questioning, I had some good friends, including Heather Floyd and Terry Jones, two kids living in Norman who would play a big part in my life in years to come. I had a steady boyfriend, Doug, who stood by me and was always ready to listen, and as my high school years unfolded, I was discovering something just as exciting, challenging, and fulfilling as basketball had been.

As I said, music had always been in the background of my life, and not just on Sunday morning. My dad was a country music fan, partial to Merle Haggard, and it seemed like all my aunts and uncles played one kind of musical instrument or another, and at family re-unions, impromptu bands would spring up as everyone got out their fiddles and guitars and just about anything else that could make a tune.

With all that music around me, it was only natural that when I started showing an interest in singing and performing, I had more than enough encouragement to give it a try. I also seemed to have enough talent to make the effort worthwhile, and when I was sixteen I started taking voice lessons from a wonderful teacher in town.

Often, lying in bed at night or just daydreaming in class, I would cast my thoughts into the future and imagine what I might like to do with the rest of my life. That dream, more often than not, featured me as the next Sandi Patty, but I told myself I had to be realistic. It seemed like teaching music was something that might have real rewards—not only would I be involved in a profession that would give me creative satisfaction, but I'd also have the chance to give a part of myself back to people. Even at that age, I had the feeling that doing things for others, finding a way to be of service, was a way to achieve contentment and fulfillment in myself.

After my junior year in high school, I began seriously thinking about college, and just as naturally, I assumed I'd be attending Oklahoma Baptist University. After all, that's where my dad had gone, and there were still plaques in the school's hall of fame with his name and basketball records on them. My oldest sister had just graduated from OBU and had been involved in a choral group called the Little Sisters, which was sort of an auxiliary to the men's chorus. It seemed like fun and, more important, Oklahoma Baptist was a school where, because my dad and sister had gone there, I would be welcomed with open arms.

All of which goes to show you that just when you think you've got life all figured out, God comes up with a new game plan. A friend of mine strongly urged me to check out a school near Hot Springs, Arkansas. The name just stuck in my head, even though I'd been telling everyone for five years that I would be going to Oklahoma Baptist.

Since my family was planning a spring break vacation at a Hot Springs resort anyway, my parents suggested that I go down and audition for Ouachita's music program while they spent some time relaxing in a borrowed motor home and my dad got in a few rounds of golf. As it turned out, Ouachita was to be the first stop on the wonderful journey my life was about to take.

I'll never forget walking into that audition room. There were four teachers there to evaluate me, and from the very first moment, everything seemed so right. I'd already been on a tour of the campus, which was spacious and beautiful, and I just couldn't get over the feeling that this was exactly where I belonged.

That sure wasn't the feeling I got later that week when, on the way back from vacation, we stopped by Oklahoma Baptist, where I'd arranged for another audition. In contrast with Ouachita, where everyone was warm and friendly, this school felt big and impersonal. Knowing my sister and dad had gone to school there, I had it in my head that it would feel like a second home. But when I got there, it seemed to me I was just going to be a tadpole in a big pond. Of course, Oklahoma Baptist is a great school, but I think the reception I got was just God's way of making my choice as cut-and-dried as I needed it to be.

It didn't even matter so much that I didn't get the biggest music scholarship at Ouachita that year, which went instead to a young upstart named Shelley Phillips! Seriously, though, Shelley, who is one of the funniest people I've ever known, was one of the first people I met at Ouachita and was soon to become one of my best friends.

I was so busy right off the bat, I didn't have time to worry about making an impression. It was hard leaving home for the first time, especially for my mother, who, after all, was watching her last baby leave the nest. I was a long way from the familiar streets of Norman, a long way from the safety and security of a home and church that had meant so much to me, but I also had this unshakable notion that I was doing the right thing.

Of course, making the adjustment to college life wasn't exactly easy either. My first roommate, another music major, was a nice enough girl, but she was totally different from me, with the habit of burning strong, musky-smelling incense that filled the room with eye-burning smoke. During those early months I think what got me through was the fact that, more than anything, I wanted to avoid conflict. Come to think of it, I'm still that way: I'll do anything to make sure things work with someone, even if it personally puts me out. I'm not sure if that's such a good trait in every situation, but as far as that smelly smoke was concerned, I was determined not to make a fuss.

But in other situations, well . . . I just couldn't help myself. I'd already determined that I was going to give up basketball in college, and it wasn't too long after arriving at Ouachita that I got completely engulfed in my studies and extracurricular activities that make up the world of a music major. No one even knew that I'd once been into sports until one of the social clubs I'd joined went out for some intramural basketball games.

When I suited up and rolled out onto the court that first time it was like I'd never been away. I guess the part of me that is naturally competitive took charge and I got a little carried away because when one of the girls on the other team got hold of the ball and wouldn't let go, I yanked it out of her hands and knocked her down. I got a real kick out of seeing the look in people's eyes as I strode off the court that day. I wasn't quite the demure little Oklahoma girl everyone had imagined.

That first year at Ouachita was one of the most exciting in my life. I got involved in everything you could possibly sign up for, talked to everyone who would give me the time of day, and rarely got into bed before two o'clock, before jumping out of the dorm at eight in the morning for my first class. It's funny when I think back on those days, now. After all the traveling I've done with the group, all the late nights on the tour bus, I always try to grab a few hours of sleep whenever I can. But in those days I was really burning the candle at both ends.

Staying busy was also a way for me to keep from getting homesick. Whenever I started getting a twinge of it, I turned to my friends. It was during that period that I got really close to Shelley, who would later become my roommate. Like I said, God was making moves in my life, even though at the time, all I knew was that I'd met a great girl who was friendly and funny and a talented singer.

Among all the activities that filled my days and nights the one I enjoyed the most was being part of the Ouachitones, a singing and performing group consisting of fourteen girls that would put on shows and concerts almost every weekend.

I was the hostess of the Tiger Tunes, our school's annual variety show, which entailed arranging a lot of the songs and accompanying choreography. The experience really helped me to sharpen my stage skills. There was also a lot of planning and production to take care of, and there were times when I really had to exercise authority in making sure people got to rehearsals and followed the routines we had worked out. Leadership didn't come naturally to me, but when I was forced to take on the role, I did it with 100 percent commitment. One way or another, I was getting the security and confidence I'd been lacking since my days on the basketball court.

Getting so involved in performing, was the perfect training for what would come later. Once again, it seemed like God was gently but firmly leading me in the direction He wanted me to take, without me even knowing it.

Within the Ouachitones were smaller vocal groups, and one of them was a trio that included me, Heather, and Terry. Now, the fact that we were all from Norman, had gone to high school together, and had all ended up at Ouachita was another one of those godly coincidences that, in retrospect, revealed His plan. We weren't all that close as friends growing up, and even after arriving at the same college, it took a while for the three of us to find each other. When we did it was, not surprisingly, through singing. We slowly discovered that we liked the same kind of music, that our voices blended well together, and, most important, that we liked each other as people. So, I guess it was only natural that we were in complete agreement when the next step presented itself.

It seems to me as though those college years just flew by. I was always busy with classes, concerts, and social club events, and before I knew it, I was in the first semester of my senior year and all set to realize my ambitions to teach music. I had job possibilities all lined up after graduation, but I couldn't quite get this little voice out of my head that kept saying, "Is this really what you want to do?" The problem was, even if I wasn't sure, I didn't exactly have any other options to exercise.

All that changed one afternoon in the front pew of a church where the Ouachitones were scheduled for an evening performance. Heather, Terry, and I had just finished our sound check and were sitting there with nothing much to do, when the guy behind us running the sound board casually leaned forward and said, "Y'all are good. The three of you ought to do somethin' together."

It wasn't the first time we'd heard that suggestion: as part of both the Ouachitones and the Tiger Tunes, we'd heard more than once that our voices had a special quality, which, joined together, made something bigger and better than any of the three of us could do on our own. But there was something about that particular moment; something in the timing or our mood or maybe just the looming prospect of graduation and what was waiting for us after the cap and gown. Whatever it was, it seemed to pass between the three of us like an unspoken promise. I don't know who thought of it first, who said it first, or who was the first to agree, but suddenly we had decided that we'd take the upcoming summer to sing together and see what would come of it.

For me, I think the idea wasn't so much more than maybe singing at a few of the summer camps for churches where the Ouachitones sometimes performed to help out with the school's recruitment drives. Yet, I could tell by the look that passed between us that day, that this was serious . . . we were going to give it our best shot. But God wasn't quite finished. Back at the dorm room that night, I excitedly told Shelley about our plans to form a trio for the summer and she asked, "How about making it a quartet?" Suddenly that seemed as natural and as right as our original notion.

I remember lying in bed that night after lights out, with all sorts of thoughts, dreams, and prayers drifting through my head. Singing onstage was, without a doubt, the most exciting and satisfying thing I had ever done in my life . . . next to scoring with a winning basket in the final seconds of a tight game. I knew that, if I could do anything with my life, singing would be it. However, until that moment, it had just seemed like a dream that would always remain the glimpse of another life that I might once have led. I prayed that night with a clarity and purpose that was new to me. "Lord, you know what I feel in my heart about all this. You know what I want, but you also know that, no matter what, it's your will that I'm seeking for my life. If you want me to teach, then I want to be the best teacher I can be. But, if you want something else for my life, please show me clearly what it is and give me a whole heart to follow the path you've laid out."

And that's exactly what He did. It's funny, but the thing that struck me the most about putting the group together that summer wasn't the way our voices seemed to mesh so well; and it wasn't the way that people seemed to respond so to us, giving us the encouragement that confirmed our decision to keep going.

What really stuck out for me was how well the four of us got along. As much as our music was the product of our distinct voices, our group was also the result of four distinct personalities, each with her unique strengths and weaknesses, and each with something special to offer. There's no denying that we're all very different people, but anyone who's been around us for any length of time will tell you that, together, we form a strong bond that's as much about respect and admiration as it is about who takes what lead vocal part.

It was during this time that the sense of depression and anxiety, that gnawing feeling of not really knowing who I was, seemed to fade and relax its grip on my spirit and mind. I really was doing something that felt so right. Of course, it's not as though I'm never plagued by self-doubt. More than once I'd wince if I sang a few notes off-key during a solo. I felt, in those moments, that it was now more than just myself I was disappointing: it was the other girls in the group and the audience that had come to see us. I wanted so much to live up to everyone's expectations, and I guess I always will. But, like I said, part of growing up and discovering God's will is realizing that His perfection is all you need. Do your best, and he'll take care of the rest.

Music wasn't the only thing I had to trust God for during this time either. During my first year at Ouachita, I broke up with my high school sweetheart, Doug, and although I dated occasionally through the rest of college, I often wondered whether I'd ever find somebody who I could really consider spending the rest

of my life with. Doug was such a close friend and con-
fidant, and there had been many times when I'd wondered whether we would get married. But we just
weren't meant to be, especially after I went off to college and our lives began to go in different directions. I
eventually got serious about another guy who had a
wonderful family, and the same thoughts went through
my head, as I guess they do with every girl: "I wonder
what it would be like to wear his ring on my finger?"

Like everything else in life, however, surprises come
whether or not they're part of your neat little agenda.
Anyone who thinks that God doesn't have a plan for
their lives, or that His plan isn't worked out to the last
detail and final quirky coincidence, only needs to look
at what's happened to me to be convinced otherwise.
No matter where I thought I was going—toward a life
as a professional basketball player, a music teacher, or
a free-and-easy college girl with no ties to bind—He
had other, better plans in mind.

I got the first inkling of the difference between His
way and my way of doing things on a fateful summer
day between my junior and senior years. The serious
relationship I'd been developing came to an end when
we realized that we just weren't right for each other,
and I promised myself, "No more guys for the time
being!" To take my mind off of my faltering social life
I took a few summer school classes at a local junior
college in Oklahoma City and was just finishing them
when I casually agreed to meet a guy for lunch . . .
nothing serious, just a break from my busy routine with
a fellow student.

Anyway, his last class ran longer than mine and while I was waiting for him I happened to pass by the administration office. I glanced into an opened doorway, and inside was someone I'd never seen before. He was kind of cute, but what really struck me was the expression on his face: complete frustration. I could see he needed help, so I asked him if there was anything I could do. He just looked at me and blurted out, "For the last two hours I've been trying to enroll in a scuba diving course here and I've been run around to at least twenty different offices!"

I laughed and pointed him in the right direction, but he suddenly didn't seem so interested in finding that class. He asked me where I was from and what school I went to. We soon discovered we had a few mutual friends and both loved basketball and some other incidentals that maybe by themselves didn't add up to much but together made a conversation that lasted a half hour.

Well, right in the middle of this fascinating encounter, my original lunch date showed up, and the three of us ended up eating together. I guess the guys were sort of confused about what the other one was doing there.

As far as I was concerned, there was no doubt: neither one of them was the man of my dreams. After lunch I went home, thinking nothing more about my chance encounter until a few days later when I got an unexpected phone call from the frustrated scuba diver. I hadn't given him my phone number, only my name, but he'd tracked me down and asked me out on a date.

I agreed, and that night, playing putt-putt at the local

miniature golf course and each trying to keep our respective natural competitive urges under control, I really got to know Stu for the first time. He was very easy to talk with, and he not only shared openly about his life but also was genuinely interested in mine. I went from just being polite to finding myself really drawn to this honest and sincere guy, with a great wit and sense of humor.

He was from Oklahoma City, from a divorced family, and hadn't really seen much of his dad growing up. Most of his formative years had been spent with his mother, who never remarried, and his younger brother. Considering his rough beginning, it was only by God's grace that Stu became the guy I suddenly found myself so attracted to.

He had a few close Christian friends and his parents always made sure he went to church. But it was really just between him and God when, at the age of nine, Stu kneeled down and asked Jesus into his life. Ever since that time he's never doubted his faith or God's love for him.

But Stu is hardly the kind of guy who waits around for someone else to make his life happen. He got a job as a firefighter at a very young age and paid his own way through college. He was the youngest member ever to join the Oklahoma City fire department, and later, when he made a move into the medical field, training for work in an emergency room, he took hold of that decision the way he does everything else . . . firmly and without letting go.

I suppose you could say he took hold of me with

both hands, too. After that first night, we continued dating for the next year and a half, talking for hours on the phone when we couldn't be together, getting to know, and love, each other more and more.

In the meantime, of course, I completed school and started working on our singing group. Stu was working just as hard at being a firefighter but soon realized he wanted to try something new and began attending medical school at the University of Oklahoma to get a degree as a physician's associate. He subsequently landed a job and applied himself to it with the same energy and determination he puts into everything.

It was on New Year's Eve 1991 that he surprised me with a beautiful engagement ring that he'd picked out all by himself (with a few pointers from Shelley). Because of our touring schedule we had to wait awhile before we actually got married. When our wedding day finally did come, what made it even more special was that it fell on my parents' thirty-third wedding anniversary.

By the time Stu and I had been married about six months, Point Of Grace had really taken off. We'd signed a recording contract with Word Records, the Christian record company that releases our albums. The company was urging us to relocate to Nashville to be closer to the studio where we'd record the album, as well as being more in touch with the music business in general.

For the other girls, the move was an exciting one; Nashville was the big time, a city full of music and musicians, and moving there was real proof that we had arrived. But, for me, making such a move wasn't something I could decide on my own, and to be honest, I just wasn't sure how Stu would feel about it.

Hindsight, they say, is perfect, and I think now that there was never any question that Stu would have agreed to go. But I sure didn't know that when I swallowed the lump in my throat and put the question to him one evening. His response, to me, says everything about the sort of person my husband is, and the reason why I love him so much. "I can see that God is working in your life," he said. "And I can see that He's doing something through the group and your music. Of course we'll move." I was so grateful for his unqualified support. What I appreciated even more was my husband's positive outlook and enthusiastic approach to life. He's a person who knows how to make the best of a situation and rises to challenges with energy and optimism that never fail to amaze and impress me.

I was relieved, of course, and tremendously grateful, but I think if we had known how difficult the coming days were really going to be, we both might have had second thoughts. For one thing, Stu had to finish his rotations or he'd lose out on his certificate and all his studies would have gone to waste.

So we took a trip to Nashville to find a place to live. It was really an act of faith, mainly because we had made the move on the hope that the one job Stu had been offered, the one that would allow him to finish his training, would actually be there when we arrived. It was, and we both saw that as an encouraging sign from God that we were doing the right thing.

The other girls had all moved down about a month

earlier and had found a place to live together. At first I was so relieved about Stu's job situation that I didn't notice that I was feeling a little left out in my relationship with the girls. It was different being the only one married. Not that anyone meant it to be, it was just that Shelley, Heather, and Terry were now living together and planning things such as how to decorate their kitchen or whatever else, and I was spending my time with Stu.

Because of my natural tendency not to make waves, it wasn't easy sharing my feelings, but one day I broke down in the car and told them I was having a hard time adjusting to everything. They were so sweet and really listened to what I had to say. Shelley even sent me a card that I still keep inside one of my Bibles reminding me of how special our friendship is.

About the same time, we developed our own unbreakable rule: if something comes up that affects us as a group—whether it's the choice of a song, whether to go out on tour, or even what we wear onstage—if we don't have a unanimous vote, we reject it. That's the only way we could find to bring together four such different personalities. Most of the time it works just fine.

Of course, democracy isn't exactly possible, or preferable, in a marriage. One partner can always veto another, and it sometimes seems like everything you do has a consequence, one way or the other, on the person you've chosen to share your life with.

For Stu and me, adjusting to married life was made a whole lot more challenging by the work I was doing. After we finished our first record, the group went on the most extensive tour of our career, sometimes leaving home for twenty-two days out of the month. Stu tried his level best to understand, but if anything, it was harder on him than on me. At least I had the support of old friends and the distraction of working day and night. For Stu, too many of those early days consisted of coming home to an empty house in a strange town and waiting for the phone to ring with a faint call from his faraway wife. It was a loneliness I shared, too, no matter how busy I was with the group. The truth was, I missed him terribly.

Sometimes, it just got to be too much for him. "I'm tired of this," he'd say during those anguished calls. "Are you ever coming home?" For both of us it started to sink in just how fragmented and fractured our life was becoming.

But I can remember only one fight we ever had during those times. Through tears and angry words, we tried to sort out our feelings and it came down to one simple, but painful fact: Stu loved me too much to make me choose between him and my career. He never said as much, but that reality hung in the air between us, and I realized, in that moment, just how much I was asking from him.

I don't know any other person who would have made the sacrifices he did. I'm not even sure I would have risen to the occasion if the tables had been turned. But I do know this; because Stu was willing to give up his own comfort and convenience for the sake of something he truly believed was part of God's plan, I will never be able to take for granted his love, my marriage vows, or the life that we have promised to share together. I think that's the reason I feel so blessed and happy to be married to such a wonderful guy. Stu has taught me about the reality of love and commitment, but more than that, he's just a great person to be around. I've always cherished his good nature and great sense of humor and the way he makes even the most routine things in life seem fun.

Well, as they have a tendency to do, things eventually sorted themselves out . . . or at least one set of problems was replaced by another set. And through it all, God has remained so faithful. As Point Of Grace continues to grow and find new audiences, somehow I find the time to be home more. It's as if making Stu and my marriage a priority actually creates more time to devote to them both.

Which, I guess, brings me full circle. If I've learned anything over the years it's that being yourself means listening to your heart, discovering what's most important to you, and pursuing it. Along with that also has come the discovery that where you find your self-worth is among your friends and family, the circle of people who love you and support you just for who you are.

I've struggled a lot with my image; the one other people see and my own self-image, and while that struggle still continues, I know what God means when He says He loves us. It's the real us He's talking about, the one that only He knows!

DENISE JONES

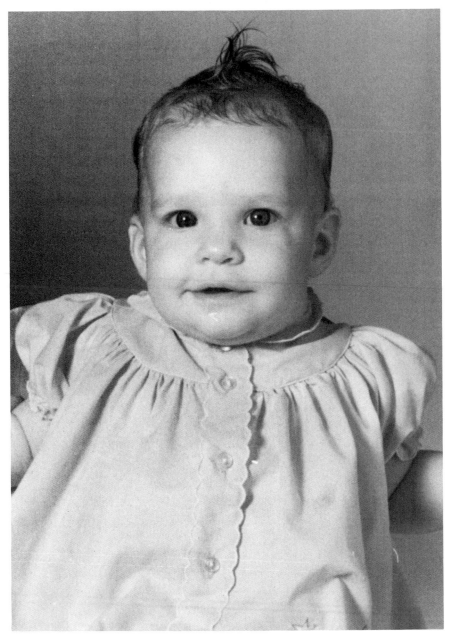

Denise Radon Masters, 6 months.

Easter, 1970. My father and me, in my Sunday best—including patent leather purse and pumps.

Sisters. Donita, me, and Dayna. (It's a good thing for Donita they came out with contacts.)

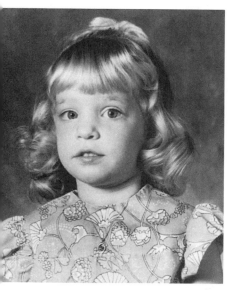

I swear I didn't do it! Here I am, looking guilty at 3½.

My family, 1977. My parents, Don and Janice, with me and my sisters. If you could choose your family, I'd choose them.

Above: Batter-up, 1986. (Aren't those the sexiest legs you've ever seen?)

Above right: Senior year basketball, 1987. I proudly carried on the family tradition, and—better yet—was able to do it with perfect hair!

First runner-up, 1987. At the local Junior Miss Pageant—I still think the wrong girl got the crown.

Stu and me at our wedding
in Norman, Oklahoma, on
September 19, 1992. The start
of a picture-perfect marriage.

Say So at the First Baptist
Houston Christmas Pageant,
1992. (We were supposed to
be Christmas Barbie dolls,
but we looked more like
Cabbage Patch Kids!)

New Artists of the Year. Point Of Grace at the Dove
Awards in 1994, wondering which of us gets to take
home the prize.

SEX, DATING ...
AND WAITING

Maybe it's because of our message of abstinence and sexual purity; maybe it's because we just try to live out our convictions about saving yourself for marriage—whatever the reason, we get more questions about sex and dating than practically any other subject (with the possible exception of how to get started in a singing career!).

The answers to those questions a lot of times aren't so easy to find. We can tell people what we believe, and why this issue is so important to us, but when it comes right down to it, everyone has to make a choice for themselves ... and live with the consequences of that choice, sometimes for the rest of their lives. Whatever answers we give, we try our best to take this into account.

But we also don't want to just stand on the sidelines, giving advice. Because we feel so strongly about sexual purity, and because of our support of organizations like Mercy Ministries, which builds homes for unwed mothers, we tell kids about saving sex for marriage, pointing out all the practical and spiritual reasons behind that decision. True Love Waits is another nationwide program we really believe in. Some kids who complete the True Love Waits course go through a ceremony and wear a promise ring that they keep on their finger until they get married, when they then offer it to their spouse. It's a real symbol of what they've done for that person. We need a lot more of that kind of commitment.

We're not trying to preach or lecture, prove a point, or win an argument. These issues make a real difference to real people . . . just like you. Talking about them is a big responsibility, and we wouldn't be completely honest if we said that, lots of times, we just don't feel up to the challenge. We're just four young women trying to be up-front about our own lives and the lessons we've learned . . . sometimes the hard way.

But, in the end, we wouldn't be honest if we didn't talk about them because we truly believe that they can make such a huge difference in the path your life might take; because sometimes it's hard to get straight answers to questions that can seem so mysterious, scary, or just plain embarrassing. We're not saying we've found all the answers (even though, with two of us married, one of us engaged, and one of us single, we've got the bases covered). What we are saying is that the answers we've found have worked for us and we hope they work for you, too.

So here's the old game of Twenty Questions with a whole new twist—sex and marriage, dating and waiting—from our point of view.

Q: What's wrong with sex before marriage?

Denise: I guess we could go through a bunch of scriptures and Bible teachings, but it all boils down to God having a set of standards and rules that He wants us to live by. One thing He tells us over and over is that sex is for marriage. It's part of His plan.

I think the reason abstinence is a big issue in America right now is basically because of fear: fear of getting diseases and getting pregnant, and, of course, all those fears are very real. But my reason for saving sex for marriage was because that's what God wanted me to do.

Shelley: When I was growing up, my parents always told me that sex before marriage was wrong. But, at that time, I think the reason that I never had sex wasn't only because of values; I was also afraid of getting pregnant. Later I realized that pregnancy wasn't the issue. What was important was what was right and wrong.

Sex is the closest you can get with somebody physically, and I wouldn't want to get married having been that close with someone else. I once heard about an eighth grade girl who said she was going to remain a virgin until she was married because she wanted her future husband to know she loved him even before they met. That's pretty profound, but it's not just for girls. It's important to us that guys save themselves, too.

Terry: It's so dangerous these days, with teen pregnancy, AIDS, and other sexually transmitted diseases. But if two people save themselves for each other, you're not going to have to worry about who your partner has had sex with before. Chris and I waited for each other, and though we didn't have to worry about those things, it was so much more than that. Sex gives us a bond that only we two share. He's my closest friend . . . in every way.

Heather: If you believe in God, then you know that He has a plan for our lives, and for some people part of that plan is marriage. That's something very sacred because you commit totally to one person; your whole life is building up to that moment. For me, I think it's going to be something very special. I've saved myself my entire life, to share myself and be intimate with someone special. Why ruin it now?

Q: Is sex sinful?

Terry: No! A big no. I think that's a hard one for kids who grew up in the church, because there they tend to make it sound so wrong. And then, when you do get married, you can't get over that connotation because you haven't heard much about the good part, when it's within a marriage.

I know when Chris and I first got married, it seemed so weird when my mom and dad came to stay with us. I felt like I shouldn't be sleeping in the same bed with my husband. Even though I knew that it was all right, it took some getting used to. Sometimes, all we hear about is sex being wrong. Which is sad. Because it's really so right when it's within the confines of a marriage.

Heather: My friends in college always used to tease me because I'd say that I couldn't wait to have sex. I will wait, but in another way, I can't wait. I know it's going to be such a special thing, because that's the way God planned it. It's all a matter of timing: it can ruin your life if you do it before you're ready.

Denise: God wouldn't have made us the way He did if it wasn't something we're supposed to enjoy. But it should be enjoyed within the boundaries He's established. Unfortunately, many kids don't know what those boundaries are. They might have grown up in single-parent families and saw their mom with a different boyfriend every night. After they've seen that over and over again, maybe they think it's not that big of a deal. Deep down inside, I think every girl dreams of being a virgin when she gets married. But what's important is whether we choose to follow that conviction. Believe me, I waited, and because I did, sex with my husband is a wonderful thing.

Q: How can I tell my boyfriend or girlfriend that I'm not ready without losing them?

Shelley: This might sound like a stock answer, but if your boyfriend is mature enough to think he's ready for sex, then he ought to be mature enough to accept the fact that you're not. I don't want to seem judgmental, but that's just a cruddy boyfriend. Do you really want to be with a guy who you're always scared of losing if you don't do what he wants?

Heather: Anyone who really loves you is going to respect the way you feel. I think that a lot of girls, especially, have lost respect for themselves. But I think if a guy respects a girl, he won't force anything. And if not, then forget it. You don't need to be with him because he won't respect you in any other way either. Who knows what he'll force you to do later on in life?

Denise: I think that if a guy really cares about you and wants to make you happy, then you can sit down and tell him how you feel and what you believe. And if he can't agree with that and support you, I don't think you have any business dating him. And if he says, "Well, if you really love me, then you would do it," I just think that's plain selfish. Love, true love, is never selfish.

Terry: I realize that guys are structured differently, and they are much more physically oriented, and I wouldn't tell a girl that if her boyfriend ever even thought about sex or mentioned it, to just get up and leave him. Chris and I talked about it. It's a struggle, but you find a way to deal with it.

Q: If sex is God's gift, why can't I open it?

Denise: Because there's a time when you will be ready for it. Waiting makes that gift even better. When you work hard at saying "no" for a long time, and you get married and you're able to say "yes," that means so much more.

Heather: I think it has a lot to do with personality. Take me, for example. I'm the kind of person that at Christmastime, I'm dying to know what gift is in that box under the tree. But then again, I would never open it because I don't want to ruin the surprise before Christmas morning. But there are other personalities. I know my grandmother, for one, is the sort who would go and unwrap it, see what it was, and then wrap it up and open it again on Christmas. There are certain people who want to have that gift now, and there are certain people who don't. Personally, I can't wait to open the gift.

Shelley: One way of looking at it is that you're opening a can of worms. Some people who have already had sex, and then decided it was wrong, think they're being good as long as they don't have sex again. Having sex makes everything else less of a big deal. If you have a good-night kiss, it's no big deal because you're not "doing it." I want my good-night kisses to be a big deal!

Q: Kissing, necking, petting . . . how far is too far?

Terry: I think I've come to the conclusion that it's an individual decision. No one can tell you how far is far enough for you. I mean, there are those on the extreme side who would say you shouldn't ever kiss before you're married. I'm sorry, but I think that's ridiculous! To never kiss somebody and then marry them would make them completely foreign to you; you'd be scared to death. So, I don't think there's anything wrong with kissing before you're married.

But there's a point in your head when you know it's

wrong, when you've gone too far because your conscience tells you so. You need to know what you can handle and what you can't. Just remember, as far as you can go emotionally, spiritually, and mentally with someone, you can go that far physically too. You just have to be careful where to draw the line.

Heather: There are lots of people who have already passed that point, who have already been physical and are trying to come back to save sex for marriage. To them I'd say, if you've messed up, you can still make the commitment, even if you've already had sex. You can still—today, right now—make that decision that you are going to save yourself for marriage, and it can still be just as special. It's never too late to start again.

Shelley: When you first date someone, it's easy to get involved really fast because of the excitement of a new relationship. So, in the beginning is when you have to have your guard up, even more than you do later. I don't know why it seems easier five or six months down the line to resist the temptation than it is in the beginning, but it's always been that way for me.

I remember a few times feeling guilty because it seemed like I'd crossed the line. I mean, I had violated my conscience and I knew it. I remember once a boyfriend asked me, "What's okay? How far is too far?" And all I could say was, "I don't know. I just know when it doesn't feel right." I want to be able to look someone in the eye after one of our shows when she asks me, "What do you do with your boyfriend?'' I want to say, truthfully and honestly, that I'm really proud of the way we act when we're by ourselves.

When you go past kissing, hugging, or cuddling, it gets really hard to turn back. That's my limit, and I've tried to stick to that. Nine times out of ten, if you put yourself in a situation where you know you're going to be alone and you're going to make out, forget it. So much of this issue is just being practical. Stay out of dark places. Set a time for yourself to be home. Find friends that feel the same way you do and struggle with the same things you do. Ask them to hold you accountable.

Q: Is "safe sex" really safe?

Denise: It's certainly not safe as far as disease goes, which is what most people mean when they're talking about safe sex. And it's not safe because of the possibility of pregnancy. But it's also not safe because emotionally and spiritually it has a big impact. Being that intimate with someone at too young an age or outside of marriage leaves you so much more open to pain. There's so much more emotional attachment.

Terry: They say that any kind of birth control is only 90 percent effective. To me safe sex is abstinence. That way you know you're not messing with anything; you're not playing with fire. It's like, if you don't take that first drink you're never going to get drunk: if you never go far enough to worry about it, you'll never have to worry.

Shelley: I think that the whole idea of safe sex shows how far we've come in society today from what's really right. Sex is safe if it's with your husband or wife, if it is done the way God intended, within the boundaries he's established. I know people are going to say, "But you know kids are going to have sex. Isn't it better to pass out condoms?" Well, sorry, but no: I'd rather we try to get to the root of the problem, to teach kids the difference between right and wrong. I don't think the solution is putting condoms in the schools. I think it's a deeper issue in the heart of a person.

Q: TV, movies, music . . . sex is everywhere. Where should I draw the line?

Denise: I know I'm guilty of going to a movie and after I got there thinking, "I should've known better!" The same with some television programs. I don't believe some of the stuff they have on TV. It just blows my mind! You have to really think about what you're listening to and what you're watching. No one's forcing us to hear or see this material.

It's true of anything that we might struggle with. If gossiping is your weakness and you hang around a certain friend who likes to run people down all the time, then you either need to be aware before you get into that conversation and plan something positive to say, or just watch how much time you spend with that person.

On the other hand, there's no use running away from the problem either. When I was growing up, I knew kids who were on drugs and who came to class high after lunch. I still tried to be nice, but I didn't want to hang out with them. You've got to know your weakness—know what you can tolerate and what you can't.

Shelley: You've got to be careful about your role models, too, the ones you want to be like. Is it some supermodel on a billboard in really tight jeans and no shirt, hugging another girl? You need to hold your standards higher than the world around you. Don't get down in the mud with them.

Of course, I know there are people who might think I was wrong for watching the show *Friends* because it's got a lesbian couple on it. I don't personally agree: we can't alienate ourselves so completely from what's going on around us, especially when you're in the position that we are in this group. If we're ignorant of what the people in our audience are watching and hearing, they're going to think we don't have one hip bone in our bodies. I've got to be able to talk to that girl after a concert and say, "Oh, you have a haircut just like Rachel's," and hopefully the girl will think that she can be normal and have a clue who Rachel is and still serve Jesus.

Heather: I'm one of the world's worst when it comes to movies and television. I see a trailer and it may be for an R-rated movie and I say to myself, "Wow, that looks good! I really want to go and it probably isn't really that bad . . . just the language or something." In moments like that you have to make a decision, you have to think ahead: am I going to feel bad if I see that movie and there's something in it that's not going to do me any good? Still, while I've walked out on movies, you can't just walk out on life.

We're all going to make mistakes, but we can pick ourselves up and learn from those failures. You see a movie you shouldn't have seen, so the next time you know. For instance, there are people who would dog us because we saw *Legends of the Fall*, which is an R-rated movie. Well, that's a decision we made and if they're going to judge us, they're going to judge us. But always remember, when they're pointing that finger at you, there are three fingers pointing back at them. You may think that's a silly statement, but it's true.

Terry: When I was in high school and college, my thoughts were very black and white: "Do this. Do not do this." And it saved me from experimenting with drugs and alcohol or going to parties where I shouldn't have been. I just never did it, which was probably a really good thing, especially in high school, because you're so easily swayed by friends and what they do.

When you're younger, it's okay to have firm boundaries. If you have to stay home with your parents on a Friday night and watch TV, well, maybe that's not the coolest thing to do, but in five years nobody's going to care anyway. But you'll always live with the choices you made, whether you stayed home or went out and got drunk. That'll always be with you.

Also, we tend to forget sometimes, but there are laws

we're supposed to obey. If it's against the law to drink until you're twenty-one—then don't. If it's against the law to go see an R-rated movie until you're seventeen—then don't. Once you've passed that age, then it's a personal decision for which nobody else can or should be the judge.

I remember once a magazine interviewer asked us what recent movies we had seen and who our favorite actor was. I had just seen *Legends of the Fall,* so I said Brad Pitt. I added jokingly, "He's so cute," or something flip like that. Well, we got some letters. One man wrote, "I cannot believe that a member of Point Of Grace, which stands for morals and purity, is going to go see an R-rated movie! Should my thirteen-year-old girl go see this movie?" That made me really sad. I mean, you can try to live up to everyone's standards about everything, or you can just be yourself.

Q: I think I love him. How can I be sure?

Terry: I broke up with my husband two or three times when we were dating, just to be sure. But seriously, what worked for me was to wait. That's how I knew that I was in love with him. I waited and we went out, off and on—mostly on—for five years. Then it got to the point when I knew I had waited long enough, that I couldn't live without him. I knew I needed this man to complete my life. If we hadn't waited, I think we would have gone through a lot of frustration being married and maybe not even really knowing for sure if it was right.

Everything's great when you first get together, but you don't know the person well enough to realize what's going to bug you about them. Maybe they're irresponsible in this area or that, and if you wait for a while you're going to find that out. Guaranteed.

It's funny, but when we broke up my senior year, this was probably the best growing time—spiritually, emotionally, and mentally—of my entire life. Being away from him for a year and a half helped me to figure out what was important to me. He wasn't there to take up all my attention.

The same goes for guys: if you're not sure, when you ask a girl to marry you, that you couldn't walk next door to a pastor and say your vows, then you don't need to be giving her a ring!

Shelley: There's always been that temptation for me to say "I love you" if I'm really attracted to someone. Because that's what I think I'm feeling. But I've got a rule of thumb that says wait a little longer to make sure. It's ridiculous to say you're not going to tell him for one year, but if you think you really are in love it's not going to kill you to wait for six weeks or however long it takes until there's no question and you feel like it would work out if you were with this person forever.

I've learned that lesson the hard way. I had a boyfriend who I thought I was probably going to marry. I told him I loved him and really believed I did. Then things started to fall apart and I ended up wishing I hadn't ever said the things I did.

There's another piece of advice I'd give: don't feel

like you always have to have a boyfriend. Sure, being alone is hard. Sometimes it's just about the worst feeling. But I think that's where your faith comes in. I'm not saying just let God be your best friend and you'll never feel alone, because you will. But I think if you have His strength to lean on, and His truth to draw from, you can be content and happy with where you are.

Heather: I've thought I was in love several times and it didn't work out. I wish I knew the secret of being sure, of being able to make wise choices that aren't based on the emotion of the moment. It's so important to be clearheaded and farsighted.

I'm at the place in my life where I'd like to know the answers to the questions: How can I know if I love him? How can I know if he's the right person?

Denise: I'm not sure when you ever really know. I can remember the day before I got married, I was still asking myself, "Is this the right guy?" There are so many words for love: if you study the Scriptures in the original language you'll see the word *love* translated five different ways.

I think we really have to be careful with the word *love* in today's society; it can mean so many different things. Like the guy I dated in high school. He was my best friend. I cared for him so much and in a way I loved him.

But was it like the way I love Stu? No. The longer I've been married, the more I realize what love really means is sacrifice, commitment, and giving of yourself to another. That takes time.

When Stu and I first started dating seriously, I don't know if I loved him in the sense that I was ready to get married. But about four months before we were engaged there was a change. Inside I knew I couldn't live without him for the rest of my life. And that's the difference.

To me, really loving somebody is when you've been married thirty years and you're not all that attracted to each other sometimes and the kids are gone and it's just the two of you. Maybe you're sitting in front of the TV and you look at each other and think, "I don't feel in love right this minute, but it doesn't really matter. I'm committed." When I watched my grandfather bury his wife, my grandmother, this year, I saw love; I saw souls separated. That's the kind of love we need to strive for.

Q: He says he loves me. How can I be sure?

Shelley: Does he treat you right? He says he loves you, but do you ever feel afraid that he might leave you? Do you ever feel confused about his intentions? Do you ever feel that you're not respected? If these are questions you ask yourself about him, even though he says he loves you, he probably doesn't really.

Or maybe he loves you in the way that he thinks that love should be, but it's not satisfying to you. Ask yourself: does he make me feel secure yet at the same time let me be my own person and make up my own mind? One of my boyfriends tried to tell me it wasn't God's will that we break up. But I don't think that God sends two different signals to two different people who are supposed to be together.

Terry: It's really hard to know, because I think girls can get so confused. They dig deeper than they should into these things, while as far as guys are concerned, it might be much more casual. It may not mean as much to them sometimes. But for a girl, you want to know that it's real. You don't want to hear that he loves you and find out later that it was just because he wanted sex or felt he should say it right then. You need to watch how you treat each other. Chris, for example, plans special times, just for us, with fun places to go and new things to try. The person you're with needs to accept you for who you are, faults and all, and not always nag you to change. They should want you to be the best you can be.

Denise: A lot of girls don't even know what it feels like to be treated special. Guys should care for you and cherish you. You come first. I can see that in Stu. When we first started dating, I could see his devotion and his care, his willingness to give up things to be with me. I think that's how you know when somebody really loves you. It's by their actions, not their physical attractions.

Heather: Somebody told me a long time ago that if you really love somebody, you even love the things that you hate about them . . . those things that drive you crazy. It's that kind of unconditional love that makes the difference.

Q: Is it wrong to have sexual feelings about some-one?

Denise: Absolutely not! We're all going to have sexual feelings; that's just part of human nature. What you do with those feelings is very important. If you're feeling sexual about someone, then you need to be more careful about what you do with them and how much time you spend together. But to say we don't all have sexual feelings is to deny the way God made us.

Shelley: Let's get real! I mean, we've all had sexual feelings. It's completely normal. Still, I think there's a difference between having a sexual feeling and acting out a whole fantasy in your head.

I suppose everybody gets bored with their partner at some time in their married life and is tempted by another person, but you just don't act on that temptation. You don't look at them as a fantasy object. You turn your back on those thoughts.

Terry: I don't think it's wrong to have sexual feelings for your spouse, and it's probably not even wrong when you're not married. It's just what you do with it. You have to be smart and think practically. If I do this, what is it going to cost me? How far am I committing here? What am I saying to this person? It's a much bigger deal than people make it out to be.

All those people on TV who are so promiscuous and

act like it doesn't hurt their lives are lying to the viewers. The movies make it look so glamorous and so neat. The way the media makes you feel or think really bothers me sometimes.

There's no way that having sex does not affect you emotionally. It's not just about gratification, and I believe there's no way a person will be completely content by being promiscuous. That's why we as a group want to get out there and show the other side, a better way of life.

MEET TERRY JONES

Name: Teresa Lea Lang-Jones
Birthday: May 17, 1970
Birthplace: Marin County, California
Education: Elementary education degree, specialization in early childhood, Ouachita Baptist University
Favorite Color: Deep green
Favorite Food: My mom's manicotti; also, her chocolate chip pie
Favorite Clothing Designer: Max Studio
Favorite Book: *The Velveteen Rabbit*
Favorite Scripture: James 1:2–4
Favorite Actors: Tom Hanks, Sandra Bullock
Favorite Vocalist: Barbra Streisand
Favorite Musical Style: Pop music and instrumental music (piano, symphonies, and acoustic)
Favorite Movie: *A Christmas Story*
Favorite TV Shows: *Oprah, America's Funniest Home Videos, The Mary Tyler Moore Show* reruns
Favorite Cosmetics: MAC makeup

Favorite Perfume: Samsara and Obsession (my husband Chris's cologne)

Favorite Holiday: Christmas

Favorite Animal: Bear (my dad nicknamed me Bear when I was little) and our dog, Kennsington

Favorite Waste of Time: Shopping at great stores and being with Chris, doing nothing

Most Memorable Experience: When I was a little girl, about eight, my dad would take each one of my three sisters and me on a different Saturday of the month to wherever we wanted to go. I chose the beach. It was an overcast day and the shore was covered with pebbles. We walked and talked for a long time—about school, family, and life—just the two of us.

Most Embarrassing Experience: I was a freshman at Ouachita Baptist University and had just started dating a senior. We were walking out of the chapel with a crowd of students behind us and I slipped on the brick steps and fell. Everyone saw me and a few even came over to help me up. I was horrified.

Happiest Memory: The moment Chris proposed to me, in Central Park across from the Plaza Hotel in New York City. He was on bended knee and the sun was setting. It was beautiful.

Saddest Memory: The day my dad had to go to prison

Most Treasured Possession: My husband, Chris

Best Personal Quality: Honesty

Worst Personal Quality: Organization. Sometimes I push myself too hard to have it all together and make myself crazy.

Proudest Accomplishment: The time I was chosen to do a solo in the SONshine Kids Choir when I was in the second grade, because it helped me gain confidence in singing. Also, when I won the Miss OBU beauty pageant my freshman year in college, which symbolized to me a coming out of shyness and an ability to attain goals.

Greatest Ambition: To be a Christian who is real; to be a good wife, to love my family, and one day to be a mom

Guilty Pleasure: Chocolate cake, chocolate chip cookies (without nuts)

Highest Ideal: To have perspective in life; to keep my priorities in line; to appreciate my family, my life, and what I do

"Into every life a little rain must fall"; "Every cloud has a silver lining"; "No pain, no gain." I guess we've all heard those clichés, trying to make sense of the misfortune, trouble, and tragedy that are part of every life.

I know that at one time or another I've heard them all, but when it comes right down to it, the words that I'll always remember, the ones that really do give me hope in hopeless situations and the ability to put adversity and affliction into an eternal perspective, come straight from the Bible: "Know then, that all things work together for good to those who love God and are called according to His purpose." (Romans 8:28)

All things. There have been times I've wondered how that could possibly be true: how suffering and injustice and loneliness could ever work together for good.

But there have been just as many times when I've seen God's will come to pass in exactly that way: when sorrow has been turned to joy, tragedy to triumph, and bitterness to bountiful blessings. It's happened for me, for my family, and for the people I love. And that's why the theme of my life story will always be one of thankfulness and gratitude.

Maybe you're wondering what could possibly have happened to a clean-cut girl from the California suburbs that qualifies her to claim that promise from God's word. Well, it's true that I've never been seriously sick, that my parents are alive and well, that I have a loving husband, a great job, and some wonderful friends.

But that doesn't mean that I've never had a reason to cry or to ask "Why?" It doesn't mean that I haven't wondered how life can be so unfair or if God really cares. The Bible also says that everyone has their own cross to bear, and for me, that cross has sometimes been more than I thought I could carry.

People say I'm a very emotional person, and it's true. I can cry at the drop of a hat and clean out a whole box of Kleenex at a sad movie like *Mr. Holland's Opus* or *Sense and Sensibility*. And no matter how often I think back on the hard times my family and I have been through, I'm moved to tears. But those tears aren't just about sorrow and self-pity. What overcomes me is the overwhelming reality of God's love and tender care, the way He took us through a valley of shadows and up to a brilliant vista where we could see things from His point of view and understand, for the first time, His master plan.

Sure, everyone has to go through the tough times so they can appreciate it when the good ones roll around, but for me, it's about so much more than some old saying. It's about God's incredible grace and about how, if we let Him, He will take the broken parts of our lives and make them good as new.

My life got off to a great start, May 17, 1970, in the sunny little community of Novato in Marin County, California, just across the bridge from San Francisco. That's where I lived for the first thirteen years of my life. I'm the second oldest of four daughters, with Katie a year and a half older than me, Christie a year and a half younger, and Angie, the baby, born four years after me. To this day I'm extremely close to my sisters. They are three of the most precious people I know, and I'm so proud of what they've done with their lives. I think from the very beginning, I've had a sense of security and safety that came from the closeness of our family.

Looking back on those early years, it seems we must have met every requirement for your average American household. But, even then, God's hand was on us in some remarkable ways. I was seven years old when my mom and dad were driving Katie, Christie, Angie, and me home from family camp and heard us singing the Christian songs we'd learned there. Mom asked us if we wanted to receive Jesus, and when we eagerly agreed, Dad pulled over to the side of the road. There, in a grove of majestic redwoods, he led us in prayer.

Three years later I had occasion to see God's protection and provision firsthand when I went to a county fair and my parents let Katie and me run off to ride on the Ferris wheel.

As we were standing in line, the back of one of the heavy, wrought iron chairs on the wheel broke loose and came plunging down, hitting me in the head and knocking me out, into the arms of the man standing behind us. My sister panicked at the sight of the blood all over my clothes, but the man calmly told her to go find my parents and meet us at the first aid trailer.

By the time my mom and dad came along, the man had me lying down and had stopped the bleeding with ice packs. An ambulance roared up, and in the confusion, the good Samaritan slipped away.

It was the narrowest of escapes, and it was only later that I found out I easily could have died or suffered permanent brain damage. At the hospital, where I got fifty-six stitches in my head, my parents tried to find out who had helped me, and quite possibly saved my life. The man had left his name and the phone number of the San Francisco Fire Department, but when they called, no one had ever heard of him.

An angel in disguise? To this day, you couldn't convince my parents otherwise, just as they're sure that

God miraculously healed me in the hospital when, after the doctors diagnosed me with a fractured skull, nothing broken showed up on the X ray the next day.

My dad was a very important person in my young life, a man of great strength of character and real integrity. He was and continues to be well respected and hardworking. He also had accomplished a great deal by the time he started raising a family. Popular in high school, he was both an honor student and a natural-born leader. He attended the Air Force Academy and was at the top of his class militarily, as well as playing both defensive and offensive lineman on the academy's football team. He joined the Air Force and went on, during his six years as a pilot, to become the youngest aircraft commander in the history of his unit.

After getting out of the service, he became the co-founder of a real estate investment firm that quickly became one of the leaders in that industry. He was also named president of a national real estate investment association.

A hard worker and a dedicated father, he made sure we were well provided for, with a house near a country club golf course and a shiny silver Porsche, which he used to drive around the neighborhood, with us kids sticking our heads out the top. We had vacations every summer, either to Mexico, and our ski cabin in the California mountains, or once even to Europe. There were always lots of presents under our tree at Christmas. Maybe we were a bit spoiled, but even my strong-willed sister Christie knew she couldn't get away with too much. It was, in short, the ideal of a normal and well-adjusted family, down to the doting grandparents. Some of my friends even called us The Brady Bunch. One of my earliest memories is of sitting on my grandpa's knee by the shore of a lakeside resort as he pretended to pull lemon drops from my ear. I was amazed—my grandpa seemed so magical.

As a student I worked hard to apply myself, and always did well in school. It seems like my whole life I've been drawn to music, whether it was Top 40 hits or the songs we sang in Sunday school. Shaun Cassidy was my favorite teen idol, and with my neighborhood friends Julie and Stacia, we'd make up dances to his records. In between times I listened to Christian artists like Evie, the Sweet Comfort Band, and Keith Green along with lots of Neil Diamond—all on eight-track tapes. Remember them?

I loved arts and crafts and going to movies every weekend. If you had seen me playing in front of my house in those days, there would be nothing to distract you from the impression of a happy, healthy, and wholesome little girl, with life all laid out for her.

But that rosy picture was about to change, and the assurance and security I had known would dissolve like the morning mist. It happened suddenly and without warning one fateful day when I was eleven years old. That's when my mom picked us kids up from the school bus stop, and the first thing we noticed, when we got into the car, was how swollen and red her eyes were.

Kids know when things are wrong, even if they may not know exactly what it is, and as soon as I saw the look on my mother's face, I had a sinking feeling in the pit of my stomach. Did someone die? Was Daddy hurt? Those were some of the frightening thoughts that ran through my head. And that's when she looked us straight in our eyes and broke the shattering news. My father, who at the time was running a successful real estate investment firm, was going to be sent to prison.

I couldn't believe what I was hearing. In my small world, daddies came home from work at the end of the day, read their papers, watched sports on TV in the evening, sat down at the head of the table, and tucked their little girls into bed at night with a kiss. Daddies were strong and wise and always there for you if you skinned your knee or fell off your bike or just wanted to know why the sky was blue. Daddies didn't get into trouble like this, go to prison, and leave their families all alone.

But that's exactly what was happening, and even as I listened to my mother as she explained what had happened, fear and uncertainty began to cloud my imagination. Would he ever come home? Who would be there to protect us? I barely heard my mom's words and understood even less as she told us that my dad had been found guilty of business fraud—something about false advertising—and had been sentenced to a year in prison, with five additional years of probation.

I remember, more than anything else, feeling shocked by the news. I guess I was also more than a little confused: only bad people went to prison and I knew that my dad was not a bad person. I don't think I totally understood what was happening, and when my parents told me not to worry, that everything was going to be okay, I believed them and tried to be brave.

But father or no father, there was a household to run and everyday routines that had to be maintained. In a way I think that helped us all to cope: none of us girls wanted to do anything to make life more difficult for my mother, and consequently we worked even harder to get along and stay on our best behavior. We all missed our dad terribly, but fortunately the news of our problems didn't spread beyond our closest friends, and I was spared the shame of pointing fingers and prying eyes at school and around the neighborhood.

In the months that followed, we tried hard to keep up appearances. On the weekends, my mom would drive us the seven hours it took to get to Lompoc, California, where my dad was serving his time at a minimum security prison. She tried to make an adventure of it, packing picnic lunches and staying at motels, and eventually a friend made a motor home available for us to use for the trip down and back. But during our visits, when we sat outside in the prison's visitors' area and talked, I could see that my dad was changing. He was sad and angry and ashamed all at the same time, and though I still loved him and needed him, it was hard to see that look in his eye, as if he realized that our image of him would never be the same again.

Yet through all that upset and upheaval, my parents hung in there. They had become strong Christians five years before, when my dad had prayed to receive Jesus at a meeting in Arrowhead Springs, California, and my mom had read the famous testimony by Chuck Colson,

Born Again. I'm sure it was their faith and trust in God that kept them going. Divorce was never an option because my parents were committed to each other and to their marriage, so while it was painful for us kids to see them separated, it was also reassuring to realize that this wasn't going to tear them apart.

People who know my story sometimes ask me what, exactly, my father did to land in such hot water, and if he was guilty of the crime. Well, because I was so young I never quite understood the real nature of the wrongdoing, but as to his guilt or innocence, I have to say that he was responsible for what happened. If there's one thing I've learned from this, and so many other experiences, it's that I'm not qualified to judge anyone.

We all make mistakes, even if we don't always have to account for them right away. My dad, as they say, paid his debt to society, and in the end is still a good and decent man, sadder maybe, but certainly wiser. I think my admiration for his character only grew stronger during those times.

His year-long sentence was shortened to four months for good behavior, and when he returned to us, it seemed for a moment like the nightmare was over and everything would go back to normal. But it was really only the beginning of a long journey that would have more than its share of unfortunate twists and turns.

After prison, my parents wanted more than anything else to make a fresh start, and what better way than to pull up stakes and find a place to start all over again?

And so, when I was thirteen, in the middle of my eighth grade year, we moved halfway across the country to Norman, Oklahoma.

What might have been a refreshing change of scenery for my mom and dad was a wrenching shift for me, coming, as it did, on the heels of such a traumatic event. I had friends in Marin County; I knew every park, movie theater, and mall. The last thing I wanted was to be uprooted and transplanted in a strange new place, full of strange new faces.

We drove out to Oklahoma on New Year's Eve, 1984, and spent the celebratory evening in a roadside hotel. When we arrived in town the next day, my first look at Norman confirmed my worst fears. The town had suffered a terrible ice storm the night before, the roads were slick and deserted, and all the trees looked dead and withered. It was the ugliest place I'd ever seen.

We moved into a white Colonial house in the country, a place that seemed big and spooky to me the first time I laid eyes on it. It was also empty, since we didn't have any furniture for the first couple of days. I had gotten the flu on the way out and was just about as sick, tired, and scared as I'd ever been. We all felt very lonely, being out there in the middle of nowhere, surrounded by low, dry rolling hills that were so different from the lush green mountains and valleys of Marin County.

But if the scenery was a shock, it was nothing compared to my first day at school. It was a little place way out in the country called Lake View School. I'd come from California, where everyone was encouraged to do their own thing. We dressed how we liked, walked and talked how we liked, and no one put us down for trying to be individuals.

But here in Oklahoma, everyone seemed to have been pressed out of the same cookie cutter, with midwestern accents so thick I could barely understand them. Every girl in the hallway seemed to be wearing a Polo shirt, Levi's, white Keds, and carrying a Coach purse. "Are you kidding?" I wanted to scream. "Don't you know you all look the same?"

At church all the kids seemed to belong to some clique or club that wouldn't let you in unless you knew the rules. The contradiction was they also wouldn't let you in on the rules.

I think there's nothing worse than that feeling of being alone in a crowded room, of having no one to talk to and nothing to say. I was already trying my best to get over the isolation that had come with my father's time in prison, and for me, Norman, Oklahoma, was its own kind of prison sentence. I hated going to church, I hated going to school, and I hated sitting in my bedroom all by myself, staring out at the endless country sky. It didn't seem as though there was anyone I could share my feelings with: although we didn't try to hide what was going on with my dad, it wasn't something that came up in conversation either. I was trapped, and it was during those lonely first days that I made myself a promise: I decided that if I ever saw a stranger like me walk through the doors of a church or a classroom, that I'd be the first one up to say hello. I didn't want anyone to feel as alone as I did, and to this day, I try and remain true to that vow.

Eventually I found my place in that environment, and after the initial jolt, I even started making moves to fit in by buying my own white Keds and Levi's. But I never really had a chance to make myself comfortable before the rug was once again pulled out from under our family. And this time, things would not be set right quite as easily as before.

The reason that my parents had decided on moving to Oklahoma was that my dad had found a great opportunity with a real estate company that was located in Oklahoma City, not far from Norman. What he didn't know was that this company had for some time been under investigation by the federal government for crooked dealings. He was walking right out of the frying pan and into the fire.

We weren't in Norman for more than a year when the results of the government probe came through and the president of my dad's company was indicted for illegal business practices. Because of his own background, my dad was one of the first to come under suspicion.

I could tell you that, this time around, he had nothing to do with the crimes. I could tell you that it was completely guilt by association that made him a suspect. I could tell you that as sure as I am that he paid for his past mistakes, this time he was being falsely accused. I could tell you all kinds of things, but I won't bother. Because no matter what they say, it's much harder to prove your innocence than it is for someone else to presume your guilt. My father had been convicted and sentenced for a crime he did commit. Now the same thing was about to happen for crimes he had nothing to do with.

The next few years, from the ninth grade to my junior year in high school, were a blur of frantic activity as my dad tried to fight back against the charges brought against him. Things got even worse when the trial started and my mom and dad would have to be down at the courthouse all day, rushing back to feed us and then get us to bed. Part of me wanted to know how things were going with the trial and whether or not they felt optimistic about the outcome. But there was another part that was just plain frightened, that wanted this terrible ordeal to be over. Whenever I saw those deep, dark circles of sleeplessness under my mom's eyes a little voice in the back of my head said, "It's better not to know," and so I just went through the motions, going to school, going out with my friends, doing my homework, or just staring out the window.

I don't know how much longer we could have kept that up, but one morning my mom woke us up and told us that the verdict was going to be read. Did we want to be there when the news came? "It could be a good thing, but maybe not," she cautioned. "It's up to you if you want to come along." I knew then that no matter how painful it might be, I had to be there for this family crisis.

I held my breath when the judge told my dad to stand for the reading of the verdict. His Honor cleared his throat and slowly—so slowly—studied the papers in front of him. Then, in a low, solemn voice, he announced his decision: "Guilty." A wave of despair swept over me, leaving me limp and sick to my stomach. It was a terrible nightmare that I couldn't escape.

I heard my mom's sharp gasp next to me, and I think Christie began wailing. The room seemed to be swimming, and all I could see was the figure of my father, his strong, handsome face pale and drawn, his hands gripping the edges of the table with white knuckles.

But the blows weren't over. Just when it seemed that things couldn't possibly get worse, the judge leaned forward in his chair to pronounce the sentence. As the judge's words echoed throughout the courtroom it felt as if he had torn the heart right out of our entire family. Whatever we had gone through before would be nothing compared to this. Whatever strength we had drawn on the first time could never be enough to carry us through now. My dad was going to prison for five years, with no possibility of parole.

Five years! That seemed like an eternity, and I felt as if I was falling away from everything I had once known, watching my former life disappear down a dark and dangerous hole. It was a feeling that would stay with me for a long time, no matter how much my mother tried to reassure us and soften the pain of my father's absence. It was a feeling I would become very familiar with, a deep sense of isolation that settled on my heart and mind and set me apart from the rest of the world.

You might be wondering, just about now, what possible lesson God was trying to teach us with that terrible sentence. How could we possibly trust Him after He had allowed my father to be sent away again, this time for so long, and all for a crime that he didn't commit? Is this the loving and caring God I've been talking about, the one who "works all things together for good"? How could anything good come from tearing a father away from his family and leaving them alone to provide for themselves?

I'm not sure I know the answers to all those questions, even now, nine years later. And I know I didn't have a clue as we drove home that afternoon from the courthouse, my face pressed against the car window, my eyes filled with tears. My dad hadn't even been allowed to come back with us to get his clothes. They just handcuffed him and marched him out of the court, right past us, his eyes turning sadly to each of us.

But even that same day, God began to pick up the pieces, to pull us back together and provide the resources we would need to survive. The first thing I remember happening was my mom herding us into the house and sitting us down at the kitchen table. "All right," she said, and I didn't hear even a waver in her voice. "Your dad has to be away for a long time. We're going to be on our own for now, and that means we're all going to have to try extra hard to keep things running. Your dad and I have talked about the possibility of this day, and we've come up with a plan. I'm going to start working and you girls are going to stay in school and get part-time jobs to help make ends meet." She stopped and looked each one of us straight in the eye, one after the other. "We're going to make it as a family," she said. "And we're going to stick together." Although I was only sixteen at the time, I suddenly felt like I had to grow up and do my part to keep the family intact.

It was a side of my mother I had never really seen. That day it was like she became a pillar that held up the roof over our heads, a powerhouse of energy and optimism that would sustain us through the dark days ahead. My mom is a small person, only five foot three, but just then, she took on the stature of a giant. Up until then I had always seen her as a mother and housewife, loving and gentle, but dependent on my father's strength. She loved telling us the story of how she and my dad met; he was in the Air Force and she was a waitress working in Hawaii on summer vacation from college. It seemed like her whole life was wrapped up in being a good wife to her husband and a good mother to us kids. But now, she would have to be so much more, and it was amazing for me to see her take up that load without a second thought. It was one of the first lessons God was teaching us: I believe you just don't know how strong you are until your strength is truly tested. Now, when I hear about families breaking up because of hard times or bad luck, I'm a little skeptical. I know from experience that there's nothing a family can't go through if that love and commitment is there.

During this period of time I think my personality really took shape, and even though I had to be tough and strong, there was still a tenderhearted, very emotional and sensitive person that needed to express herself from time to time. I was the same person who used to cry at Road Runner cartoons whenever the coyote got hurt.

Of course, we had no time to sit around thinking about our plight. We were struggling so hard just to keep our heads above water. But even then, in those days when all that really seemed to matter was how to get the next meal on the table, God was present and prepared.

I said that there's nothing a loving family can't get through, but that's not totally true. Everyone needs help now and again, and the help that came to us at that time was all the proof I'll ever need that God works through the love and kindness of ordinary people.

The same church that had seemed so strange and unfriendly suddenly became a source of kindness and compassion. My mom's first order of business was to get a job, and the church leadership wasted no time in offering her a secretarial position. I can't remember a single occasion when anyone at the church pointed a finger of blame or shame at us. In fact, on several weekends they'd get together a busload from the congregation to drive up to the minimum security prison where my dad had been sent, and the church members all played softball with my father and the other inmates. Denise and Heather came on those weekends. A friend from the congregation volunteered to give us girls free haircuts and perms at her shop whenever we needed them, and on the holidays they'd turn up with a full Christmas dinner with all the trimmings.

Money was tight, but somehow there was always enough to pay the bills. I did my best to keep up my end, working as a secretary, baby-sitter, full-time nanny, or anything else I could find during summer vacations. My sisters and I were each given a few dollars a week for lunch, and whenever the electric or the water bill was overdue, an anonymous gift of cash for just the right amount always turned up in the mail box.

My grandparents helped out with clothing, so we always had something nice to wear. Even though we might have had to hand down a dress from sister to sister, we never lacked a warm coat or a new summer outfit. We had to share bedrooms, two girls in each, which I didn't mind but my younger sisters hated. Then again, what kid doesn't want their own space? The fact was that during this time we really began to draw close as a family. I really got to be best friends with my sisters, I think, because we were really the only ones who could understand what the other one was going through. We talked about life, read the Bible together, prayed every night together before bed about the issues in each of our lives, and formed a bond that has stayed strong and true to this day. When I think about all the families we knew who fell apart because of a prison experience, I know that it was God who was keeping us together. Every Sunday, after church, we'd go up to see my dad, returning in time for the evening service. It was all part of keeping those ties as strong as we could, no matter what the circumstance.

All in all, it seems that we had about as normal a life as could be expected under the circumstances, thanks to the generosity and kindness of the people around us. Even in the hardest times, we still managed to have some fun. More than once I was able to take ski trips with my youth group and once went on a trip to Washington, D.C., as part of a Christian youth convention.

But, at the same time, I don't want to make it sound like everything was ideal either. After all, I was looking at the next five years—my last two years of high school and right into my second year of college—without a father at home to guide, advise, and provide for me. It wasn't easy, and I don't think God meant it to be. It was during that time that I think He established a discipline in my life and an ability to see beyond my own wants and needs that was to serve me so well in the years to come.

But there were also those wonderful times when my dad would get a pass to visit us on special occasions, like on Christmas day, my high school graduation, and later, when I was in college and had been selected as a contestant in the Miss Arkansas pageant. It was a very special time for me, made even more memorable by seeing him in the audience that night. As part of the competition I sang "Happy Days Are Here Again." It seemed to symbolize the hope that a new day might dawn for us, too. I had that same hope when I was crowned homecoming queen at college. My dad was living in a halfway house at the time, prior to coming home for good, and he got permission to come to the school and escort me on the football field.

First and foremost, I wanted to be a responsible daughter, someone my mom knew she could depend on. Almost from the day that prison sentence was read I said to myself, "I'm going to have enough grief with my dad being gone. I don't need to be creating more problems with drinking, drugs, or sex. I'm gonna make sure I don't mess up . . . too much is riding on how I act."

As a result, I think my mom trusted me with more freedom a lot earlier than she normally might have. Whenever possible, she let me make my own choices, although sometimes having to make those choices was the last thing I wanted to do. I'd be going out with my friends and she would tell me to be home at midnight. Well, midnight would come around and I'd call, begging for another hour to finish our bowling game or whatever it might be. She'd listen and then calmly say, "Well, honey, you decide what's right." I'd feel so guilty I usually just came home: I'd rather have her just say "yes" or "no," but in the long run I think it taught me how to make wise decisions, even when I didn't especially want to.

Being forced to grow up so fast also had an effect on my social life. I had a few close girlfriends, but most of the people I got close to were guys. One of my very best buddies in high school was a big, hefty Indian guy who I felt I could share anything with. The truth of the matter was that I just liked being around guys and not necessarily for romantic reasons. I could never tolerate the catty way some girls acted, which was a tendency I guess I inherited from my mom. She has always been very honest and straightforward and never stood for any backstabbing gossip. The guys I knew just weren't into that: they'd tell you what they thought about you, right to your face. You might not have liked it, but at least you knew where you stood.

As far as I was concerned, simple friendships with guys were about as far as I was willing to go. I didn't date much in high school, maybe once or twice a month, and when I did I was really picky about who I'd go out with. I had some very definite ideas about what was right and wrong, and as a result, I think I earned a reputation as being more than a little narrow-minded. But I really didn't care. As far as I was concerned, if boys were going to let me know where they stood, I was going to let them know, right back. In the end, it was that attitude that helped keep me out of trouble.

That was also a period of time when I really threw myself into the Bible, wanting to know God and find out what living a Christian life was all about. We had family Bible studies, and I went to every youth group meeting and event that was scheduled at the church. One of the biggest influences during that time in my life, in fact, was our youth leader, Steve Bushey. He really protected me and my sisters, acting as a mentor, almost like a father figure, during that difficult time. He also guided us into all kinds of activities to keep us growing in faith.

For me, the Bible was like a life preserver thrown to a drowning person: I clung to it desperately as the only thing that could make any sense out of what was happening to me and my family. I got in the habit of reading just for myself every evening, and whenever I found a verse that seemed to speak directly to my situation I'd try to commit it to memory.

One of my favorite verses, and one I learned by heart, was in James, where it says, "Consider it all joy, my brethren, when you encounter various trials, knowing that the testing of your faith produces endurance and let endurance have its perfect result that it will make you perfect and complete, lacking in nothing." That word *trial* just jumped out at me, and every time I read it I could picture that judge sitting behind his bench, pounding down his gavel in judgment of my father. The funny thing was, that verse was the very same one that both my mom and my dad so often quoted to themselves to get them through their own dark times. They'd come upon it separately, and years later when I found out, it struck me as so beautiful and touching that God was hearing the same heartfelt prayer from all three of us.

These days, when I hear about kids going through hard times, it's not so hard for me to understand why they might turn to drugs or alcohol or even join a gang. You feel like you're falling and you want to grab on to something, anything that will stop that plunge into despair. Whatever's there is what you'll take hold of. For me, it was God.

There was something else that helped get me through and that gave me pride in what I could do as well. I mentioned that music was an important part of my life from as early as I can remember, and its significance for me continued to grow as I grew older and the world's horizons began to slowly expand beyond Norman, Oklahoma.

I was still listening to the radio after school, occasionally recording my favorite songs, hits by Chicago, Neil Diamond, and others on a small tape deck I had. In school, I had gotten together with two girlfriends, Marti and Wendy, to form a country music trio called, of all things, Harmonic Balance. We thought we were pretty cool, especially after we got invited to sing at a few functions around town. Sometimes we even sang regularly at a local place called the Oklahoma Opry.

It didn't take long for me to figure out that I really loved performing, and I looked for any available opportunity to sing. Even though I was still timid and shy, I could compensate for those feelings by singing out loud and clear. I joined the school show choir, which really helped build my confidence with its singing and dancing routines, but the truth was I didn't need much encouragement. Ever since I was little and my parents trotted me out to sing in front of company, there was something about being onstage that I just naturally gravitated toward.

Singing kept me busy and my mind off my doubts and hurts. I also realized early on that God had gifted me with a vocal ability, and ever since the second grade I'd been in one sort of choral group or another. I can remember, back in California, belting out my favorite numbers from *Annie*. The little orphan was my hero, and I'd been to see the musical so many times that I learned all the songs by heart. In fact, I'm still a huge fan of Broadway musicals and catch one whenever I'm in New York City.

When I was in the sixth grade, my sister Christie and I started taking voice lessons from a hippie guy in Marin County, and when Dad first went to prison we made a recording for him on the hippie's tape deck of some Amy Grant songs—"My Father's Eyes" and "Thy Word."

But for all my interest in music and performing, I don't think I once gave a thought to a career onstage. In fact, by the time I'd graduated from Norman High, in 1988, I had pretty much mapped out the rest of my life. I guess I was always like that, responsible and organized, because I always knew I had to keep my side of the family boat afloat. I had already determined that I was going to be a teacher, because I love children and that's what my mom had done at one time.

Teaching is still a goal I hope one day to realize. I really love little children and finding ways to express my creative side, which I think are two essential requirements for the job. For me, teaching wasn't just an easy way to get a degree, as so many people these days seem to think. I wanted to get into elementary education because I believe that teachers can and do have a great impact on children, greater sometimes than any other individual in their lives. I can't imagine a more rewarding job than that.

But I think that the truth behind my choices at that time went a little deeper. As I've said, I've always been a shy person, and in my first couple of jobs it was hard to feel comfortable around people. When I was fourteen

I manned a concession stand at Oklahoma University football games and later was a bus girl at Crockett's Smoke House in Norman. But it was always difficult for me to face strangers one-on-one and harder still to get over that sense that I had stepped outside my bounds and left myself exposed. It may seem strange that someone who likes to perform in front of crowds could be painfully shy at the same time, but I think for people like me, performing is a way to come out of our shell.

In my senior class I had been voted "Most Polite" and "Most Friendly" and had participated in student government. As a result, when it came time to hand out scholarships, I was on the list. I received what they call a Leadership Scholarship from Ouachita Baptist University in Arkansas, which to me was sort of funny because I really considered myself, in years past, anything but a leader. But I was determined that I would give Ouachita my best effort.

Even with the scholarship, however, it was going to be difficult to afford the tuition at this small, private college. That's when, I believe, God stepped into my circumstances yet again, this time in the form of a friend of my parents, a wealthy woman who offered to pay my entire tuition, along with that of my sister Katie.

From the moment I first laid eyes on the campus at Ouachita, I felt comfortable. It was a small but beautiful campus, with red brick buildings, trees, and lots of pretty little gardens. Everyone from the teachers to my fellow freshman students seemed friendly and considerate. I could hear a small, but very clear voice in my head saying, "If you don't take this moment to discover yourself and let others discover you, it may not come around again. This is Terry's chance."

And it was. College was a great confidence builder for me. In my first year I was named Miss O.B.U. and the next year was crowned homecoming queen, with my dad right by my side. I was making friends, doing well in class, and finding out all sorts of new facets about my personality and my talents. Even though I'd hitch a ride from Denise for the six-hour trip home to Norman as often as I could, I felt as if, for the first time, I was offered the chance to be on my own and find out what my life was all about. I was discovering a world more exciting and challenging than I ever could have expected.

With the opportunity to sing and perform in the Ouachitones, I got to sing with two other Norman natives, Denise and Heather. We'd had only a casual acquaintance back home, where we had been at the same high school, but now we found a lot of common ground in our mutual love for music and a common belief that, come what may, we all wanted to realize God's full potential for our lives.

It wasn't long before we were performing together as a trio. Then we talked about singing over the coming summer together. It seemed like a natural next step. It was when Denise's roommate, another singer and natural born show-off named Shelley Phillips, asked to join up that we really felt we had the makings of something unique. Well, little did we know.

We called ourselves Say So, taken from verse two of Psalm 107, one of our favorites, which says, "Let the redeemed of the Lord say so." At first it all seemed like a kind of do-it-yourself project. Shelley booked our concerts, Denise picked our songs and got arrangements together, Heather was in charge of putting up posters announcing our shows, and I took care of the money. A good friend and supporter of ours gave us five hundred dollars to get things going, which was a small fortune for four college students. We printed some brochures, business cards, and stationery with Say So emblazoned on the top.

Our first performance was at a doctors' banquet in town, where we sang some Sandi Patti and First Call songs and our a cappella version of "Great Is Thy Faithfulness." In the end we got paid twenty-five dollars each. It was our first professional engagement ever.

From there, the bookings just kept on coming, and before I knew it, the summer was over and I was back in school. Throughout my senior year we kept at it, doing shows almost every weekend, building a word-of-mouth following and just trying to have as much fun as possible without really thinking about where it was all heading.

Prior to all this, my dad was finally released from prison, after thirty-nine months of incarceration. Despite the "no parole" ruling, he got out early for good behavior. It was great to have Heather and Denise as understanding friends during my dad's time away. They even came with the Ouachitones to sing at his prison chapel service. Their support and acceptance came to mean so much to me as I continued to build my self-confidence and self-esteem.

My dad had changed a lot during his years away from home. He had made a thorough study of the Bible, and it was as if God had given him a new lease on life, with a tender heart to go along with it. I remember that I'd sometimes find him alone crying, and I'd add to those moments my own tears—not of sadness, but of joy at a long overdue family reunion.

What God was trying to teach him must have had to do with pride and a broken spirit. I've never asked him directly about it; all I know is that here was a man who had everything taken away from him: his family, his livelihood, and his freedom. I think it all happened so that just at the point when there was nothing left of himself that he could count on, God stepped in and revealed Himself in a way that maybe my dad could never have seen before. Sometimes it's incredible what God has to do to get our attention.

It was wonderful to see my parents back together again, picking up where they'd left off so long ago, but I could also see that things were never going to be the same again. My father's whole motivation in life was different now, and strange as it seems, all he really wanted to do was to find a way to be of service to other people. You'd think that a man who had spent so much time in prison would have a lot of delayed desires to catch up on, but God's grace had worked powerfully in my dad, and that work, in turn, made him want to help others as he had been helped, to realize that God works for the good in every situation.

It wasn't long before my dad had an opportunity to put his newfound commitment into action. He was appointed executive director of Bill Glass Ministries, which is based in Dallas and works with prison inmates. It was one more incredible result of God's plan that through his years of suffering, he would be able to help others who were in the same position. My mom became part of the ministry, too, eventually leaving her job and devoting her time to working side by side with my dad. After everything we had been through, all the questions and doubts, God's design for our family was beginning to make itself clear.

Meanwhile, the group continued to grow by leaps and bounds. We discovered the name Say So was already being used, so we had to pick another. We found what we were looking for in a line by the famous Christian author C. S. Lewis, who had written the *Chronicles of Narnia* and other wonderful, faith-building books. He had said that "We as Christians live every day at the point of God's grace." We were now, officially, Point Of Grace.

It was all very exciting, all very challenging, and all more than any of us could have possibly imagined back in the choir in Norman, Oklahoma. But even as the reality of our blossoming success began to sink in, I knew that there was another part of me waiting to be fulfilled. When those two separate aspects of my life finally came together, they also came dangerously close to canceling each other out.

I first met Chris Jones when we were both in the same freshman biology class at Ouachita. I guess the first thing that impressed me was his size. My dad is six foot four, I've got cousins who come in well over six foot six, and I've always been partial to tall guys. Well, Chris was six foot eight and every inch an athlete, the star player on his high school basketball team with a scholarship for the Ouachita basketball team. And, if his size wasn't enough, he was also great-looking, strong, and athletic, with brown hair and big blue eyes.

Of course, as Miss Ouachita that year, I was feeling pretty confident, too. But from the very beginning, there was more between Chris and me than a popularity contest. I remember seeing him, sitting two seats in front of me in class, and wondering, "What is it about this guy?"

I've always put a high premium on honesty and loyalty, qualities that only come from really knowing someone and having a deep commitment to them. And whatever the quality was that I saw in this great guy on that first day, I knew I wanted to get to know him even better.

Not that I let him know this, at least not right away. It seemed like most guys in college would give you the time of day only if they thought they could date you, and although it seemed to me a pretty shallow way of judging people, I still accepted almost every offer that came my way. I dated a lot at Ouachita, some weeks almost every night, sometimes two or three dates a night, as part of my campaign to come out of my shell. I've got to admit, I really enjoyed the attention. But even with my whirlwind social calendar, it felt like I was missing something . . . that feeling of deep, abiding friendship that I'd had with my few best guy buddies in high school. Chris was the first person I'd met in my new world who seemed like he might be able to meet that need.

I found out later he felt the same way, the first time he saw me walking through the campus in a white minidress. He thought to himself, "I'm gonna date that girl," and at the first opportunity he arranged for us to do some studying together. Chris, I discovered, wasn't like the other guys I was dating. He was in no hurry to rush things along and really took the time to get to know who I was. My first instincts had been right: here were the makings of a true friendship.

After about a month of studying together, he got up the nerve to ask me out on a real date. Well, that first evening out was an absolute disaster. He'd gotten tickets for a Bobby Brown concert and invited me to come, but I didn't want to appear too available. So I hemmed and hawed and played hard to get. Before I knew it he was telling me he'd find someone else to go with. Well, this guy knew how to play me. I insisted that he take me and I knew we'd have a great time together.

And we did, if not exactly in the way we expected. When we arrived at the concert, Chris went to the bathroom, and while I was waiting for him some guy who'd had a little too much to drink came sauntering through the lobby and tried to pick me up, whispering liquor-soaked nothings into my ear.

I tried to get rid of this unwanted intrusion by telling him that my six-foot-eight boyfriend was coming back any minute. I don't think he believed me until Chris rounded the corner and only then did he take off to find someone else to bother.

The whole incident unnerved me, and though we watched most of the concert, I asked Chris to take me back home before it was over. That's when the trouble really started. As we were walking to the car, eight guys in a solid line headed for us. Now, you know when you meet someone in your path on the sidewalk and one of you has to move aside to let the other by? Well, these guys weren't giving up an inch of ground, and as Chris and I tried to squeeze by, one of them grabbed a gold chain that my grandmother had given me right off my neck.

I told Chris and he turned around and faced the gang. "Which one of you guys stole my girlfriend's necklace?" Before I knew it, they had jumped him and they were all on the ground. It was eight against one, but I had the feeling Chris could take care of himself. What really worried me was that some of these creeps would turn their attention on me. But before I could even think about what to do, a policeman ran up. The gang scattered, pursued by the policeman, who ran one of them down. I was asked if he was the one who took the necklace, but I couldn't be sure. All I wanted was to get out of there.

Even after that episode, our debut date still wasn't over. As we drove back in the Trans-Am he had borrowed from his sister for the evening, a dog suddenly ran out onto the road, and Chris had to swerve like he was drunk to avoid squashing the poor animal flat. As we sped on back, trying to make the dorm curfew, a patrolman happened to be watching and pulled us over. After we explained the night we'd been through, the policeman just smiled and said, "I'm not going to add any more trouble to your evening. Y'all just get on home."

And so we tried, but within a mile of the dorm the Trans-Am began to just belch smoke, stuttering and gasping. When Chris pulled to the curb, the car died completely. "Uh, maybe you should just walk on back to the dorms while I try to get this car back," he muttered, looking at the warning lights blinking on the dash. "What? In the middle of the night?" I said. I was so dazed and bewildered by the whole night, I just got out of the car and walked off.

As I headed up toward the front door of the dorms, I heard Chris run up behind me. I could see the embarrassment written all over his face, and suddenly I wasn't so upset anymore. "I'm so sorry about tonight," he said. "Promise you won't tell anyone, because if this gets out my whole life is gonna be ruined." I felt so sorry for him I agreed to keep our little secret, then ran upstairs past my scowling dorm mom and spent the rest of the night laughing about it all with my roommate.

They say that adversity brings people together. After that awful first date, Chris and I continued to see each other, but I wasn't at all sure about our future. I was still having too good a time playing the field, seeing as many guys as my schedule would allow, and Chris was just in the crowd. At the end of our freshman year he gave me a keepsake, a little emerald necklace, and while it didn't quite make up for the loss of my grand-mother's gold chain, I thought it was sweet. For a while, we dated more or less exclusively.

By the time we returned from summer vacation, however, things had cooled off again, and I made no bones about my determination to date as many guys as I wanted. It hurt his feelings, and his pride, and once again we were on the outs.

But, like I said, Chris always knew how to get under my skin, one way or the other, and when he started going out on dates of his own, I realized how wrong I'd been. "I think I've made a mistake," I said.

None of those guys measured up to Chris's stature, and I'm not talking about just his height. He was a true friend, even when we weren't dating, always willing to listen, always on hand to help. I missed him when we weren't together. It felt like a hole had opened up in my life that only he could fill.

His love, his willing ear, and his ability to make me feel secure and appreciated—all these only grew as we got to know each other better. From the time of our first date, when he faced down that gang, being with him symbolized to me a safety and security that reached into every part of my life—emotional, spiritual, mental, and physical. He's someone who has been there for me, through the trials and the triumphs, meeting each cir-cumstance with the same rock steady faith, common sense, and sense of humor.

I guess what I'm trying to say is that with Chris I found a home. He's always been my grounding point, my reality check, allowing me to be myself and not just the perfect college queen, polished Christian singer, or whatever else people expected of me. He's honest and up-front, but also incredibly tender and thoughtful. His mom and dad brought him up well, and the fact that both sets of our parents have remained faithfully married is very significant to me.

Chris's charm and character show through in the special things he does for me: giving me a bouquet of flowers when he picks me up at the airport, putting together scavenger hunts at home, or just surprising me with new clothes or a candlelight dinner. He goes to a lot of trouble just to let me know how he feels and because he genuinely takes pleasure in seeing me happy. That's a quality you don't find every day.

We dated steadily throughout our junior and senior years, but despite our growing feelings for each other, as graduation approached and my work with the group increased, I felt myself torn. Singing and performing were so much fun . . . did I really want to get tied down to one guy right away? I wasn't so sure, and Chris picked up on my uncertainty. We decided one more time to break up. We had a pretty bad breakup, with lots of tears and hurt. It was so hard because I was losing my best friend, and a love I thought I'd never find again. It was one of the most difficult decisions I've ever made. I think it left both of us wondering what the future would be like if we couldn't be together.

It was a year and a half before we would meet up again; eighteen whirlwind months in which, even though every moment was filled with sometimes frantic activity, that hole in my soul always stayed empty whenever I thought of Chris. And I probably thought about him at least once a day, and sometimes, when I felt especially alone, at least once an hour. Slowly, as the weeks went by, a strong conviction began to grow in my heart: it was wrong for us not to be together.

So we agreed to try it again, a few tentative dates to see if our emotions were real. He was living in Little Rock at the time while I was in Nashville, working with the group. The long-distance relationship made it difficult, but we would see each other every chance we got.

Right about that time Chris had a great business opportunity to spend four months in London working with the famous insurance market Lloyd's of London. Chris has always had a very keen business sense, which is something he got from his dad, who has really lived out the American dream of starting with nothing and building his own business, in his case, a major airline company. Chris promised our relationship would handle the distance and he really held me together. That's another facet of Chris's character that serves him well: his natural leadership ability.

While I was happy for Chris and encouraged him to go for it, I had a terrible empty feeling when he kissed me for the last time on his way to the airport. That slowly dawning conviction had become a burning certainty. I lasted about two weeks before I couldn't stand it any longer. I then caught a plane and flew over the Atlantic to be with him.

Europe is such a romantic place to begin with, but I think we could have been anywhere and had the kind of storybook romance that every girl dreams of.

It was a dream that came true just before Christmas, 1993, when Point Of Grace was in New York City to perform at Carnegie Hall. Chris came up for the concert and that afternoon we went for a walk in Central Park. There, just as the sun was setting and a flock of pigeons flew over the skyline, he pulled a ring out of his pocket, got down on one knee, and asked me to marry him. It was a moment I'll never forget, the culmination of a courtship that had gone on for nearly five years and the realization of a deep love, a perfect match, and a friendship that was going to last a lifetime.   This is the part of the story, I guess, where the happy couple goes off to their vine-covered cottage, raises a bunch of kids, and lives happily ever after. Well, that wasn't exactly how things turned out for Chris and me. If I had been a normal wife, with a normal life, I'm sure adjusting to being married would have been a whole lot easier, but I was one-fourth of a successful singing group, trying to juggle a busy schedule and a whole new set of responsibilities. I almost didn't make it.

Within a few months of our May wedding, Point Of Grace was busier than we had ever been, and I think we all got to feeling pretty overwhelmed by the demands on our time and energy. It seemed like we never had a minute to breathe, much less to do something nice just for ourselves or find a minute to reconnect with the people who were important in our lives. Being on the road six days a week is fine when you're foot-loose and fancy-free, but now that I was a married woman the strain was really beginning to show.

It didn't help when, because of his job working for

his father's airline business, Chris had to remain in Little Rock. Moving away from Nashville isolated me from the rest of the group and kept me out of the decision-making process, not to mention the extra burden of having to fly in every time we needed to rehearse or have a business meeting.

Things came to a head around the time when we were recording our second album. The song we were scheduled to cut was "Gather at the River," and that day the girls were irritated with me because, after a month and a half away from home, I had taken some time off and hadn't been there earlier.

Well, it was one of the worst fights we ever had and as close as I ever came to calling it quits. We might have all walked out then and there, except we'd already booked the studio time. So we sat down together, argued, reasoned, and just generally cleared the air. In the end, each of us was able to say we were sorry, hug, cry, and then, as we had done so often before, we buckled down and got to work, putting on our headphones and waiting for our cue to start singing.

We were avoiding each other's eyes when the first verse of the song came around: "Somctimes we don't see eye to eye. We don't agree and we don't know why . . ." It was like we were singing it to each other. Everything that we'd been through, as individuals and as a group, came back in a rush, and with all those recollections, the realization that no matter how difficult the problem or seemingly impossible the resolution, God had always been there for us. If He wouldn't give up on us, how could we give up on each other?

I think you can guess the end of the story. We've managed, through cooperation and mutual respect, to find a way to divide our time between home and career, and in the process, we've grown even closer as friends. My priorities in life have never been clearer: God, my husband, family, and my musical ministry, and every day I try my best to give my best to all four. When I think of all the blessings that I've received, through good times and bad, it's the very least I can do.

TERRY JONES

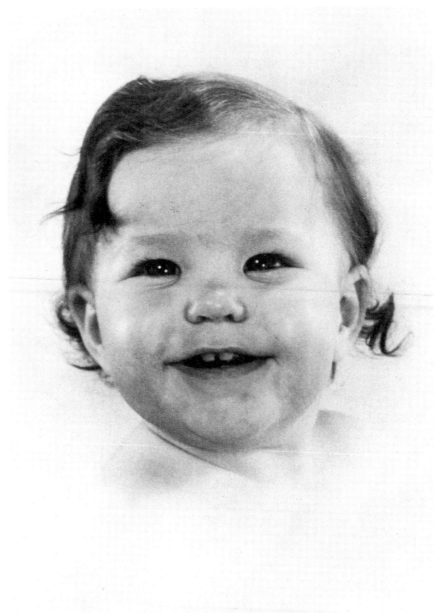

Theresa Lea Lang, 9 months.

Daddy and me after a long day at Disneyland in 1973.

Christmas Day, 1974. Practicing to be a real mommy.

Age 11, at the height of my rainbow-and-unicorn phase.

The Lang women in Paris, on our summer tour of Europe in 1981.

Skiing with
my sisters
on Mammoth
Mountain,
California,
in 1983.

A very happy family
portrait, 1986.

Homecoming queen, 1990.
Dad escorted me on the
field at O.B.U. on this
special day.

Say So at the 1992 Texas
Youth Evangelism
Conference. (Since then
we have a new name,
and smaller hair.)

Chris and me at our
wedding reception,
on May 14, 1994.

Christmas '95. My sisters and
brothers-in-law in Katie's
backyard in San Diego. Top
row: Christie, Me, Angie, and
Katie. Bottom row: Christie's
husband, Craig, Chris, and
Katie's husband, John.

My boys. Chris and me
with our dog, Kennsington.
Isn't he cute?

GET DOWN WITH YOUR REAL SELF

You've heard the saying "image is everything." In our line of work, it sometimes seems so true. We're in the business of looking our best, sounding our best, and being on our best behavior, sometimes for twenty-four hours a day, seven days a week. And that's not easy, we can tell you.

When audiences see us onstage, when we're interviewed for newspapers, magazines, or TV, when we meet fans after a show or just walking down the street, often that image is the only impression we'll get to make. There's no time for them to get to really know us, who we are after the spotlight dims and we change out of our stage clothes into sweatpants and T-shirts. That's a part of us that we can share only with those we're close to and comfortable with—our husbands and boyfriends, our friends and family, and each other.

While the truth is that our private lives are just as real as anything we present to the public, it's also a fact that with us what you see really is what you get. We don't try to pretend to be something we're not, put on airs or cop an attitude. Our image is as close to who we really are as we can make it, and we'd hope, if you

101

ever got the chance to come over and hang out with us, that the image you came in with was the one you went home with.

In other words, what works for us is being real. And that's a tried-and-true test no matter who you are or what you do. Being yourself and accepting yourself is like finding that perfect outfit: it fits right, it feels right, and it doesn't cost more than you can afford.

Unfortunately, these days, finding your own identity is like looking through one of those mail-order catalogs: there are so many styles, so many choices, so much to try . . . and buy. And, more often than not, when it finally comes in the mail, it's not what you had in mind at all.

So how do you go about discovering who you are and creating an image that reflects your own unique qualities? How can you be an individual and still find a place in the crowd? What is the secret to being comfortable, confident, and in control of your life?

It all comes down to making choices. It seems that from the moment we're out of diapers, we start imagining what we'll be "when we grow up." Firefighter, nurse, astronaut, CEO . . . it seems like whatever we want to be will be as easy as picking a hat off a rack.

But as we get older, the hard facts have a way of pushing aside all our youthful dreams and ambitions. What was once a wide-open world of possibilities becomes a cramped room filled with expectations, responsibilities, and limitations. No wonder we sometimes feel like the song says, "Stop the world! I want to get off!"

But that's only half the story. Choosing a career, figuring out how you can best use your talents and abilities and making the most of the gifts God has given you can be exciting, rewarding, and, yes, even fun, if you follow some simple rules.

Rule number one: Don't let the pressure get to you. Remember, God has a plan for your life and He's going to reveal it to you if you're patient and persistent.

Rule number two: Don't let anyone else decide for you. It's your life and with it comes the opportunity to find true purpose and fulfillment in a way that is unique to you.

Rule number three: Allow room for surprises. Maybe you've always thought you're going to live an ordinary life. But maybe God has something extraordinary in mind. You never know unless you try out lots of different options and see what shoe fits best.

Here's some other advice and experiences that we've come up with in the course of discovering who we are and what we're meant to do . . . Hope they're helpful to you in your own search.

Q: People always talk about self-esteem. How do I work on my own self-esteem?

Shelley: A practical way for anyone to nurture self-esteem is through your talents and abilities. Growing up, nobody really paid any attention to me in the seventh grade until I started singing in the choir, and I then got to do solos. Suddenly people knew who I was. That really gave me security. I could say, "I'm good at this." You've got to look for it . . . try lots of different things until something clicks. Our talent is singing for the public, but somebody who takes care of an old lady at a rest home is showing their special gift just as much.

Denise: I think when you have a good relationship with God, you begin to learn more about your gifts. God wants you to feel good about yourself. Just knowing that helps with self-esteem.

Yet we struggle with self-esteem, no matter who we are. Just the other day I was in the dressing room before a show, and as I was looking at the other performers who were part of the concert I was thinking, "Their skin's so pretty" or "They're such great vocalists," and I got so caught up believing, "Gosh, I'm not good enough to be here. I'm never going to be pretty enough. I'm never going to be talented enough."

We deal with self-esteem issues every day. But you have to remember that God gave us the qualities that make us who we are, and you have to trust that He'll show you what it is that makes you unique.

Heather: I get a lot of the good feeling I have about myself from what other people say to me. If you're around people who are always bringing you down, you're never going to feel good about yourself.

Who you pick as friends is really important, because they're the ones who can encourage you and cheer you on. It's also important to know that others need the same thing from you. They need you to say, "You know what? You're beautiful!" Or just "You look really nice today." Whether it's something big or small, everyone needs a kind word and a pat on the back once in a while.

Q: Sometimes I feel like no one understands me. Do they?

Shelly: I don't really think anyone can completely understand you, except for God. I remember when Heather broke up with a guy, she said, "I hate it when people tell you that they know how you feel! Because they really don't. Your feelings are your own."

And it's okay not to always be understood, or not to always understand other people. It's okay for me not to understand Terry, not to know why she's crying sometimes, but to love her anyway. And just because I don't understand doesn't mean I can't be there for her. Sometimes understanding isn't about talking; it's about just sitting there, listening, and being a friend.

Heather: I can remember sitting at home on my bed with my mom, and just crying my eyes out, and my mom saying, "Honey, just tell me what's wrong. If you don't tell me, I won't know how to help."

So many times I really didn't know what was wrong, but people aren't going to understand unless you help them understand. If you can open up and say, "This is what I'm going through. This is why I'm crying," then maybe a friend or a family member can be there for you.

We're all individual people with special needs, so while somebody may not understand why you're feeling the way you do, it's not because they don't want to. They may wonder, "Why in the world is she so upset? What can I do?" Give them a chance. Maybe they can relate better than you think.

Denise: A lot of times when we're upset about things, we go to our friends, or our parents, or our spouses, or go to other people, and they don't really have the answers that we're looking for. I've done that myself. But then I read in so many passages in the Bible about how God is so wonderful and tender and merciful. It's in Him that I'm going to find the comfort and support I need.

It's really cool to find something in the Bible that speaks to the situation you're in. When you find that special verse you can claim it and memorize it and it will give you a strength—something that you can hold on to. I think that's why I feel such a peace in my life sometimes, because I realize that God understands and is there for me, on my side always.

Q: I worry about what people think of me. Should I?

Terry: There's a fine line that needs to be drawn, because in some ways we should worry how people see us. I want people to know what I believe and that I try to live up to those beliefs. But then there's a part of me that says, "You know what? If I'm doing what God wants me to do and I'm acting the way God wants me to act, then I can't worry about every single thing." Of course, what we do and say matters. We have a responsibility, but it's also true that we can't please everybody. We have to do what we know is right.

Denise: I think it depends on who you're worried about impressing: is it your mom, your dad, your pastor, somebody you respect, or is it the guy that's on drugs at your school who everyone else thinks is cool? The Bible says, "Be anxious for nothing," and I don't think God wants us to worry all the time. I do think He wants us to be conscious, to live in a way that's pleasing to Him and not necessarily everyone else.

I'm the worst worrier in the world, and it doesn't do much good most of the time. When I'm conscious that God loves me and cares for me, and I'm thinking and trying to act on that assurance, it changes my focus and I'm not as concerned about disappointing people.

Q: I find myself questioning everything, even God. Is that all right?

Heather: Sure. I think everybody comes to a place in their life where they ask themselves, "Why do I believe what I believe?" You can question God, check Him out for yourself, but if you're sincere, there's a point where He's going to bring you around to believing what you knew was right in the first place.

Denise: We talk a lot about absolutes—like the absolute difference between right and wrong when it comes to saving yourself for marriage. It's because we believe that the truth God reveals in the Bible is true for all people, for all times, in all places. There has to be a standard.

But that doesn't stop us from asking questions and testing what we believe. When tragedies happen I think everyone's asked the question, "God, why did you do this? Why did you take my mother away from me?" Or even something as simple as "Why did I fail this class?"

Whatever it is, you've got to go back to the simple fact that His ways are higher than our ways. We may not get an answer right away, but maybe years later we'll understand that what we went through made us better people, more compassionate and forgiving. I think everything happens so that God can be glorified, whether we see it in our lifetimes or not.

Terry: The other day my sister was saying, "You know, I get so mad at God sometimes because I don't understand why our dad had to go to prison. I don't understand why they can't afford to send me to the college I want." She was looking for answers.

I said "You know what? God does understand. Maybe he doesn't show it to you all at once, but you've got to tell Him about it. If you keep it all bottled inside and you never ask why, then you'll just be bitter and angry. If you never go through the process of getting it out and searching for answers, then your spiritual life goes downhill. You have to work through it, talk about it, bring it to God.

Q: How can I best discover my talents and abilities?

Terry: It's a process that can start as early as elementary school. There are kids that are into sports and there are kids who want to be on the student council and others who are drawn to music or art. Discovering your gifts can start early.

Denise: I knew when I was very little that I loved sports. So to find out which ones I liked best, I tried out for every sport I could. As I got older, I focused on basketball.

But I think it's okay, at an early age, if you don't find something you're going to want to do forever. Whatever you like to spend time doing and whatever you think you're good at is what you should go for, whether it's staying home and reading a book or playing one-on-one on the court.

Heather: Finding your talent doesn't always happen right away. I've known people who started playing piano when they were thirty and turned out to be great at it. It's never too late and it's so important to dream. Without dreams there's not a lot of joy and hope in life. Of course, not all dreams come true, while others come true in unexpected ways, but you'll never know unless you allow yourself to have that dream.

Q: Do I have to choose between marriage and a career?

Denise: I think there's room for both. Stu knows that God has called me to do what I do, and he totally supports me in it. He loves me enough to say, "I'm secure in what we have together so I can let you go and pursue what God has for you."

Now, there may come a point in our lives when that won't be okay anymore. I might need to be at home more, to be a mother and a wife, and that's going to mean I have to set my career aside.

But right now I know, without a shadow of a doubt, that this is what God wants me to do. And part of knowing that is knowing there is a cost to having a career. I think Terry and I probably have to work harder at being wives when we're at home. And our husbands deserve that extra effort because what we've asked of them requires a real sacrifice.

I believe that there are people who have a special calling from God that allows them to give everything to their work. And, as a result, God gives those people a platform and an audience along with an extra special ability to handle it all.

Terry: It was completely different for me when I was dating Chris. When we got married, I thought, "Wow! I have these two huge things to juggle in my life. How am I going to balance this job with my home life? How can I show my husband my love and admiration for him when I'm not even there?" All of a sudden, I had this wonderful guy to come home to, and I didn't even have the time to be with him.

I know that God needs to be my first priority, my husband the second, and my career the third. But sometimes my career takes so much more time than either of the other two. So I try my best to get the combination right. Because if my roots aren't firmly planted, I can't go out and be what I'm supposed to be. If things aren't right with me and Chris at home, I'm not a happy camper on the road.

Q: I love music and performing. Should I pursue a career in show business?

Terry: Most of the letters we get are from people who want to do what we do. They see the exciting part of it and they really get caught up with the fun and energy and even what they see as glamour.

Growing up I never really wanted to do this for a living. It's great and I love it now that I'm in it, but I think that if you're going to go after a career in music or entertainment, you need to be really careful. Find out what it really means to live this life, being on the road and away from home so much. Make sure you've got the basic talent and that you're not wasting all your time and energy on something that isn't what God wants for you.

Heather: Go for your dreams but always have a backup plan, because nine times out of ten, making it in the music business just isn't going to happen for everyone. And for those blessed few who do make it, it's going to be very obvious when the doors of opportunity are opening and when they're not. A lot of kids say to us, "I feel like God has called me to be a singer." Well, maybe He has. It's not for us to question that call, but it's also possible it's just your own voice you're hearing.

If you want to serve people, if you want to bless them, it

doesn't necessarily have to be through music. God's calling on your life could be in any area, not just contemporary Christian music. We always tell people, bloom where you're planted. Start little and let God expand it.

Shelley: A backup plan is so important. For instance, if you're in school you don't have to major in music. We had a lot of classmates who were talented musicians, vocalists, and instrumentalists but they had different majors. One of the most talented musicians I've ever known is working today in marketing. He can sing and play the piano, but he does it now at his church.

Where we live in Nashville, there are so many wonderful artists who are really struggling, just scraping for work. In Nashville, your waiter is a bass player and your electrician is a drummer! They come here thinking they're going to make it big, and they end up with a lot of unfulfilled dreams.

Denise: I think what's most appealing to a lot of the kids is when they see the approval that we get from our audiences. It's very gratifying, but it's also a very dangerous place to be because you can start to believe what people say about you and forget that we're all equal in God's eyes. We're not any greater than anybody else. We're just out in the public eye more.

When I read your letters I sometimes want to give a warning: "Why do you want to do this? Is it for you? Or is it for God?" These are questions you should really think about because there is a lot of disappointment and rejection in this business.

Q: I'm confused by the message of women's liberation. Is it for real?

Shelley: Women's liberation has sent the message that you can have it all. Well, maybe you can, but it won't be without sacrifices and a lot of very difficult choices.

Women who want careers usually want it for the same reasons that men do: good pay, respect, prestige, and fulfillment. But they're not always willing to play by the same rules as the guys. They decide to start a family, which impacts their job performance, and then they wonder why they aren't getting the same opportunities for promotion. That's the choice they made. If women want to be treated equally, then they're going to have to realize that having a job and a family is like dividing yourself down the middle. No one really gets the whole you.

Heather: Women can do great things and we haven't always had the opportunities. I think women are called by God to a special job that men could never do as well. Today, so many moms don't have time for their kids, and that's where the family breakdown begins to happen.

Terry: In the Bible it says that wives should submit to their husbands. Yet, today, so many women, even Christians, are saying, "I shouldn't have to be submissive to my husband. I'm as much an equal partner in this marriage as he is!" That's not really the point.

Some people don't really understand what the Bible is saying about the roles of men and women. It's not about putting women in their place. To me, a women's role is always as significant as a man's role, but in a different way. God intends them to work together.

Denise: Love means serving. When you look at Jesus, you see how He loved us by becoming a servant. And by serving her husband, a woman is loving him. I know that a lot of women will say, "So you think that men can just lord over women?" No! It says in the Bible that a husband is to lay down his life for his wife. It's all about having respect for each other, and for yourself.

I think there's something innate in women that allows them to take on that servant role. At least there is in me. I want the guy to take charge, to have the last word. My mom and dad would discuss everything, but I always felt that my dad had the final say. And with that came responsibility.

People think there's something degrading about being a servant. Actually, it's a beautiful thing. How incredible it is to love somebody so much that you want to do things for them and help make it easier for them. It's not demeaning at all. It's a very fulfilling role.

MEET HEATHER FLOYD

Name: Heather Lynaye Floyd
Birthday: January 18, 1970
Birthplace: Abilene, Texas
Education: High school and three years of college (but determined to finish when I finally get the time)
Favorite Color: Red
Favorite Food: It changes: sometimes Mexican, sometimes Italian
Favorite Clothing Designer: Donna Karan
Favorite Book: *'Til We Have Faces* by C. S. Lewis
Favorite Scripture: Hebrews 11:1
Favorite Actors: Anthony Hopkins, Annette Bening
Favorite Vocalists: Nat King Cole, Billie Holiday
Favorite Musical Style: Changes with the seasons
Favorite Movie: *The Color Purple*
Favorite TV Show: *ER*
Favorite Cosmetics: MAC makeup
Favorite Perfume: Angel by Thierry Mugler

Favorite Holiday: Christmas

Favorite Animal: Darla, my Shih Tzu

Favorite Waste of Time: Movies or reading

Most Memorable Experience: When I was sixteen, my dad taught me how to drive a standard transmission car on a very steep hill. It took forever, but I finally got up that hill.

Most Embarrassing Experience: I had just bleached a pair of jeans and I wore them to my high school football game. With the entire band walking right behind me, I tripped. The inevitable happened and my jeans split open. I was devastated.

Happiest Memory: Each year, the day after Thanksgiving, my family chops down a Christmas tree. We pick out one new ornament apiece and go home to decorate the tree while listening to the same album of Christmas favorites year in and year out.

Saddest Memory: Losing both of my grandfathers to cancer

Most Treasured Possession: My Ryrie Study Bible

Best Personal Quality: Loyalty

Worst Personal Quality: Procrastination

Greatest Accomplishment: My senior voice recital in college

Greatest Ambition: To have a family just like the one I grew up in

Guilty Pleasure: Driving fast

Highest Ideal: To live a life as holy as possible

for a saved sinner, so that one day I'll hear my God say, "Well done, my good and faithful servant."

I've heard people talk about having a spiritual experience that knocked their socks off, changed their lives, and set them on the straight and narrow. Sometimes it's a vision, sometimes a voice, sometimes just the sudden realization that they've come to a crossroads where there's a life-changing choice to be made and no turning back.

I get a real thrill whenever I hear those stories. There's a verse in the Bible that talks about the angels in heaven rejoicing every time one soul is saved. It's a thought I cherish. I've been around long enough to know that God works in different ways for different people and that He'll do whatever it takes to bring someone to Him. Each story is different, but the results are all the same: lives changed, hearts softened, and old hurts healed.

And sometimes, when I hear a really dramatic story, about somebody saved from drugs or alcohol, lifted up from the gutter or pulled out of the fire at the last possible moment, I wish that I, too, had a breathtaking tale of sin and salvation to keep everyone on the edge of their seats.

But my story is different and my path to God not quite so littered with obstacles. Don't get me wrong: I've had my share of difficulty and doubts, straining to hear God and wondering if He's still interested in my life. But if I were to tell my testimony around a campfire one night, I think the results would be fewer bated breaths and wide eyes than a warm glow and a soft sigh of satisfaction. To put it simply, God has been good to me.

So good, I sometimes feel as if I should apologize for the seemingly simple life I've led. But, of course, the story doesn't stop there. God's goodness, I've often heard it said, is like a river of refreshing water. We can gather it up in a pool and drink from it whenever we're thirsty, but if we don't let that pool overflow—if we don't give his Love and blessings away to others—the water just gets stagnant and unhealthy.

For me, that's the whole idea behind Point Of Grace. God has given us a very special opportunity to share His grace and love through our music and the examples we set with our lives. If we weren't doing our job—singing these songs of praise and speaking out about the liberating power of His truth—I don't know that our lives would be empty. Maybe we'd all be happy housewives or dedicated career women in some other field.

But, like the old saying goes, "If the shoe fits, wear it." We've been given so much, through our families, our friends, and our personal journeys, and there just comes a point when you've got to give it away to get some more, to try and touch others as you've been touched. That's what our music is about . . . and that's what this book is about.

My life story may not be the next installment of an Indiana Jones film, full of hair-raising escapes and last-minute rescues, but sometimes the excitement and drama of life are wrapped up in the living it out—day by day, staying true to what you believe, and trying to make the most of the gifts you've been given.

I'll bet, when all's said and done, that there are a lot of people who have found deep meaning in their seemingly mundane existences and the realization that, in the routines of life, God works His will in miraculous ways. Maybe, like me, you're one of them.

I was born in Abilene, Texas, on January 18, 1970, in the closest hospital to the little town of Sweetwater, where my mom and dad had set up house. Two years later, my younger sister, Misti Dawn, was born and rounded out the family circle. My dad worked as a technician for the phone company, which meant we moved a lot, as he was stationed in one office after another around the country. There were brief furloughs in Roscoe and San Antonio, Texas, then Kansas City for three years, and finally Norman, Oklahoma, which is where we finally had a chance to put down some roots, settle in, and get to know the neighbors.

Actually, what we lacked in local connections we more than made up for in family bonds. My mom and dad had been boyfriend and girlfriend since the third grade and grew up in the same tiny West Texas town of Munday. One of our family treasures is a photograph in their grade school yearbook that shows my dad holding out a chair for my mom in the cafeteria. They looked so cute back then, and even today, they seem as much in love as ever. I still catch them holding hands when they're walking anywhere together, and it makes me feel great to know that love can continue to grow over a whole lifetime.

There's been a real theme of consistency and continuity in the Floyd family saga from the very beginning. My dad was nineteen years old and working at a gas station when he heard about a job opening at the phone company. Because he was smart and ambitious, he landed the job, and now, at forty-nine years old, he's just retired after thirty years with the same company. Now, in a way, it's like his life is beginning all over again. He and Mom have moved back to the small town where they were raised and live on the same farm where my mom grew up.

I don't think my dad was always overjoyed at the prospect of getting up every morning and going to the same job, and I know that, in his younger days, he had harbored a dream of going to college. But, with a young wife and two daughters, he did what he had to do: he found joy in his responsibilities and never complained or resented that his own dreams had been put on hold. To me that's the real definition of a hero.

My mom has the same gentle, soft-spoken spirit and self-sacrificing streak. She's the kindest, most tender-hearted person I know and never intentionally draws attention to herself. Whenever she'd get mad at someone, she'd mutter under her breath, "I'm going to give that so-and-so a piece of my mind." But, as far as I can remember, she never did.

It goes without saying that my mom is also one of the most loving people I've ever known. It's a quality summed up in a story she often told me. Before I was born she had miscarried twice, and when she finally got pregnant again with me, she told herself that she was going to be the happiest expectant mom alive. She wasn't going to let anything get her down. At night, while lying in bed, she used to talk to me in her womb, telling me how happy and excited she was that I was on my way. Well, it must have worked, because I was born one happy baby, smiling and cooing almost all the time.

When I think about the kind of guy I'd like to marry someday, and the kind of life I'd like to have outside the group, those qualities of stability and dependability that I had around me at home always come to mind first. Knowing what I know about being a performer, I don't think I could handle someone whose schedule is as scattered and hectic as mine.

I've learned a lot about the demands our kind of life can make on a marriage by seeing what Denise and Terry have gone through. You couldn't find two greater guys than Stu and Chris, but even they go through periods when they just get fed up with their wives being away all the time. Sometimes we have to leave seven different telephone numbers where we can be reached when we're out on the road touring . . . one for every day of the week.

I know the cliché about girls wanting to find a guy just like their dads, so you can call me typical, but I really do value the steady, calm, and totally reliable dedication that he always showed toward his family. I just hope there's a few left like him when I get ready to settle down.

Although our family moved around quite a bit, all

the different places we lived still somehow felt like home. We grew up in the kind of safe and nurturing environment that's getting harder and harder to find these days. My earliest memory is of playing with my doll Suzy in the backyard and pulling her around in her car by a string.

I also have very clear, and very precious, memories of growing up with my sister, Misti. We were very close as children. Mom used to dress us alike, and we had so many different outfits, it's like we were twins. We really enjoyed just being together, and although she was younger, Misti often provided the creative spark for our playtimes. She used to make up songs in her own language and put together costumes of the imaginary characters she'd created. She always kept me entertained and on my toes: I was never sure what she'd come up with next. But, although I was very conservative and she was always into her own thing, we formed a strong and lasting bond.

Misti had a rebellious streak from the very beginning, and it was one of the things I enjoyed most about her. She just didn't know how to conceal her feelings: Misti was up-front and honest about everything. There've been times in my life when I wished I'd had a little more of Misti's independent spirit, but there was always so much more to her than just being a rebel. Her honesty was never less than refreshing, and even today, she's the kind of person I feel I could talk to about anything. Even though she's been through some hard times in her life since our carefree childhood days, I've seen how much she's learned from her experiences, and how they've made her a wise, strong, and caring person.

But, of course, there were times when she thought I was nothing more than a Little Miss Goody Two-Shoes and refused to listen to a single piece of advice from her big sister. Well, maybe I was a little too straight and narrow, but I thank God for the early influences in my life that kept me out of trouble. The center of my social world, as well as the place where I felt like I most belonged, was in church. My best friends were the kids in my youth group, and when I'd hang out on the weekends, it was with them.

Attitudes in our church group were different from those at school or in my neighborhood. There wasn't the pressure of having to be popular, or the stigma of not fitting in. Everyone was accepted, and respected, for who they were. Being popular was never much of a concern of mine to begin with. I guess since we moved around so much, I never really had a chance to establish myself with one "in" crowd or the other, and by the time I got to Norman, it just didn't matter. Although it took me a while, I found what I was looking for: a circle of friends who shared my beliefs and were ready to take me in for who I was.

For the Floyds, church life and family life went hand in hand. Sunday morning services and Wednesday night Bible studies were a tradition, and some of my best memories are of riding through town together, arriving at church as a family and leaving the same way.

Coming home on those Sundays, my parents would ask us girls questions about what we had heard and what we had understood. It was then I realized just how much I didn't know about God, the Bible, and being a Christian. I started taking notes during the service so that I could really grasp what the pastor was saying, and when asked, I could proudly pop up with the right answer.

Of course, being a youngster, I wasn't always paying strict attention, and sometimes my mom, who sang in the choir, would have to come down and sit with me to keep me from talking with my friends. But even in those formative years I really believe that God gave me the strong desire to know Him better. And that desire has only grown as I have.

My first real encounter with God was at age nine, when we were living in Kansas City. I was at the Sunday school in the basement of the church we attended there, and the teacher, who I remember as a warm and funny guy, invited us to accept Jesus.

I think I knew exactly what I was doing, but I have to admit that I got a little scared when my mom came down to the basement classroom, crying tears of joy. It was also a little intimidating when they took me out of that basement classroom to go upstairs and sit with the grown-ups.

The second encounter is even more vivid in my memory. It was in Norman when a preacher named Bailey Smith came through during a revival time in our church. The message he brought was taken from Matthew 13, the parable of the wheat and the tares, which, in case you don't know, are weeds that look like stalks of wheat and sometimes grow up right alongside the crop.

Well, the meaning of the verses came home to me with a powerful impact as he spoke about how the tares will try to choke out the wheat, but in the end, the wheat will stand tall and firm and those weeds will wither away.

I was only twelve years old, but I knew I wanted to be counted among the stalks of wheat, being useful and nourishing to those around me. I wanted to make a positive difference with my life. I stood up and marched down the aisle, not caring who was looking or if my friends thought I was crazy. I wanted God to know I was serious about dedicating my life to Him.

Well, He took me at my word, and throughout my early teenage years I really tried my best to share the joy I was feeling with my friends at school. I invited my classmates to go to church with me, and if they didn't come I'd ask someone else. I think I realized even back then that if I was going to be any use at all, I was going to have to expand my circle of friends to include people who maybe weren't Christians yet.

I was a one-girl evangelist in middle school, and I clearly remember sitting in science class putting together my homemade battery and telling the kid next to me, "You know, Jesus is coming back. You need to get your life straight." Funny, but I didn't feel superior or judgmental or better than anyone else: I just loved God and wanted other people to know what I knew. It was simple; if you had great news, news that could make the difference between life and death, wouldn't you want to share it with everyone? I couldn't be responsible for whether or not they heard what I was saying. My job was to spread it around, like a town crier ringing a bell.

Which isn't to say that I was always operating out of the very best motivation. For instance, when I was a sophomore, I had two really good friends named Keri and Chelly. I don't think either of them were Christians at the time, but they were both the sweetest girls, and I loved hanging out with them.

Well, around this time, my Sunday school class was having a contest to see who could invite the most kids to church. We were competing against some other classes, and I really pulled out all the stops, inviting everyone and their cousin and their cousin's cousin because I wanted to win so badly.

When that Sunday rolled around my class had really packed the place out. There were kids hanging from the rafters, and among them were Keri and Chelly. As we started tallying up the count it was clear we were going to be a hands-down winner, and I felt like standing on a desktop and crowing! It was just about then that I looked across the room and saw my two friends and it hit me: "This is not the reason you should have invited Keri and Chelly here today. It's not about numbers. It's about lives."

I was so busy adding up numbers that I forgot that behind those numbers were real people, with real problems and real needs that only God could answer one-on-one. From that moment on, I promised myself that I would also meet people's needs face-to-face. Maybe I wasn't going to win the world for Jesus, but I could make the difference where it really counted, among the individuals He had put into the middle of my life.

People ask me if there was ever a moment when I doubted my faith, and while there have certainly been times when I felt God's presence stronger than others, I can honestly say that I never had a reason to believe that He wasn't on my side. Which isn't to say that I never had struggles or a reason to wonder why things didn't turn out differently. Even today, I sometimes find myself wishing I could consistently feel that fervor I had as a young Christian—on fire and ready to change the world.

These days, you hear so many conflicting versions of what true spirituality is all about. I'm always ready to listen to what other people's religions might teach, but I guess you could say my mind is made up about who God is. I have absolutely no doubt that Jesus Christ is the Son of God and that He was sent to earth as a sacrifice for our sins, died on the cross, and was raised on the third day. This is the simple, honest truth as I know it. If you don't agree with me, that's all right; maybe someday you will.

I know that, as the Bible says, we need to be as crafty as serpents and as innocent as lambs. And I take that to mean that it's not enough just to know what you believe. You've got to be able to defend those beliefs when others present a different point of view. The people I respect the most are the ones who have made a study of Hinduism and Buddhism and even atheism, not because they are on a spiritual search, but because they want to be able to talk intelligently to those who follow those faiths. One of my goals in life is to find out more about world religions so that I can really—as they used to say in school—"compare and contrast."

There's no doubt that being raised as a Christian my whole life has been a tremendous blessing. But when I look at it objectively I have to admit that there's been a bit of a disadvantage to it as well.

I've been protected from the bad things in the world, but I've also been sheltered against the reality that's all around us. Like everyone else, I hear about drugs, prostitution, gang violence, and other problems but have never really had to face them. I see it as being in a safe and warm bubble, but it's a bubble that God has been pricking and pushing in different ways as my horizons continue to expand, both as an individual and as a member of Point Of Grace.

As we travel around the country, doing concerts and meeting people, I'm beginning to see more and more of just how much I don't know. There are questions that I'm asked, hard questions that come from the hard places in people's lives, and I don't always have an answer ready. Being sure about my faith is one thing; being able to express that sureness to others is something else entirely. If I'm asked a question about abortion, abstinence, or divorce I want to be able to tell them not just what I think is right, but why. I want to be able to point them to the right Scripture, the right teaching, or even just let them know that, while I may not have the answer, there is someone who does.

And I'm getting there, one step at a time. It's not so

easy for me these days just to tell other people "God said it, I believe it, and that settles it!" I want to give them more, and the more I open myself to new ideas, and really listen to where others are coming from, the more I can be useful to the God I serve.

What I've discovered in the process is that things aren't always just black or white. Which doesn't mean that there isn't a right and wrong to every issue, only that sometimes we have to dig a little deeper.

I'll give you an example: when you search the Scriptures for the answer to a particular question, sometimes you find passages that are very clear-cut and sometimes there seems to be a lot of wiggle room.

There's a rule of thumb that I learned from Max Lucado, a friend and well-known Christian author of such inspiring books as *No Wonder They Call Him the Savior, And the Angels Were Silent,* and *On the Anvil* (all published by Word Books). Max says there's one consistent response throughout, which means that for God there's no two ways about it.

The Bible consistently teaches that God hates divorce. My own opinion is that in many situations divorce is just a sign that people have given up and taken the easy way out.

On the other hand, when it comes to the issue of women serving in the church, there are different points of view. My feeling is that there is definitely a place for women to teach, and even preach. But because the Bible isn't specific on that question, I think it means we're free to interpret the answer, based on the situation and the circumstances involved. While the solution to every single problem in human existence isn't spelled out in Scripture, there are guidelines that we can follow, using the common sense and good judgment God gave us.

When I'm onstage with Point Of Grace, it's my privilege to talk about saving sex for marriage. And part of the advice I give the kids in the audience is to think ahead and stay out of dark places. It's not like I've never been tempted to wander into those shadows myself, but I count myself blessed that, when I was young, I never felt the need to rush into growing up.

I didn't date a lot in high school, but when I did go out, I'd have tons of fun with a whole group of kids. It was so much easier that way; we could concentrate on having a good time instead of wondering how far was too far or who was doing what with whom in the backseat.

I think I was starting to realize, even back then, how important it is for everyone to find their own path to God. For me, it was easy and natural; for others it can be a struggle. But in the end I believe we can all come to the same place.

Having that closeness with God from as early as I can remember has given me a different perspective to go along with a very defined personality. People who know me will tell you that I'm definitely not a morning person and that, as far as organizational skills are concerned, I'm a basket case. But the natural happiness I felt as a baby has remained with me up until today and so has the feeling that I want to go as far as I can in pursuing God's plan for my life.

But I also believe God has given me another gift

that's really come in handy more than once. It's like I have an invisible set of feelers that start to quiver when I meet someone who I should be steering clear of. In the Bible they call that gift "discernment," and when you meet as many folks as we do from week to week and city to city it's a very positive asset to have an innate instinct about which ones are on the level and which ones you need to watch out for.

Unfortunately, my gift of discernment wasn't much help in "discerning" the answers to pop quizzes and finals at school. I tried hard but was never much more than an average student, putting most of my energies, instead, into extracurricular activities. I loved volleyball and fast pitch softball, but it was another interest that took up my time when I got into high school.

Actually, my interest in music goes back to my early childhood. Everyone in my family was musical in one way or another, and I can't remember when we didn't trade off the verses to our favorite songs or hum a catchy melody as we did the chores. Somewhere in the family archives is a tape of me singing my first solo at age five. My dad was the music minister for a revival and he had me come up and do a rendition of an old hymn called "Fill Me, Jesus." I was just a little thing, but I remember like it was yesterday walking up to the front of the church as my mom played the opening notes on the piano. "Fill me, Jesus," I belted out with a full-blown Texas accent, "fill me now. Fill me with that precious holy power. I'm yours, my Lord, to do with as you will, so fill me, Jesus, right now."

I really meant it, too. After the song was over I looked around to see if anyone else was going to come up there and sing after me. And there was my dad, nodding and smiling and saying, "Sing it again!" So I did and, to tell you the truth, I haven't stopped since.

In school, I went out for the show choir program, which included dancing as well as singing. Though dancing didn't come nearly as naturally for me as singing, I loved every minute I spent in that choir, although it was a lot of hard work.

I loved the feeling that you got when you hit that note perfectly and heard it bouncing right off the back wall. My mom and dad both have great voices, and when I was little, I was in total awe of my mom's pure, clear vibrato. I used to shake my head and rattle my voice around to get the same vibration.

As I got older and more experienced I realized that God had given me a real gift with my voice and I wanted to make the most of it. Singing on pitch, hitting those high notes, and giving the words just the right inflection was something that satisfied me like nothing else in my life, and I worked very hard to polish and perfect my talent.

I've always felt very fortunate to be doing something I love as much as singing. Whenever I find myself complaining about some small irritation, I look around at other people who are working so hard just to survive, with jobs that may not give them real fulfillment, and I count my blessings.

Which isn't to say that trying to be grateful always works. Sometimes life can just get to be overwhelming, and it's at those times that I've learned that the best way to face disappointment is straight on. I guess the biggest disappointment I had growing up was when, at sixteen, my dad bought me a beautiful Ford Mustang. I was so proud of that car and kept it in tip-top condition, tolling around town just to be seen by my friends.

Well, almost a year later, on the eve of my seventeenth birthday, Norman was hit with a heavy winter storm. My car was almost buried in a blanket of snow, so I thought I'd get a jump on getting to school the next morning by running the car to melt some of it off. I got the car idling and went back in the house to get warm, but it couldn't have been ten minutes before I saw thick black smoke drifting past the window. Because of a faulty part, my beautiful car was in flames, and I watched helplessly as it burned to a charred hulk. Needless to say, turning seventeen wasn't exactly what I'd been expecting.

Back at school, things were going well. My choir teacher took me under her wing and taught me a lot about reading music and the more technical side of the craft, and when I was in tenth grade I started taking formal voice lessons.

One of the biggest opportunities I had was being accepted as part of Oklahoma's All-State Choir. That experience really helped me put my own talent into perspective, realizing I was just one more voice in a sea of singers, many of whom seemed so much more gifted than I was. I felt lucky just to be there, working with a repertoire that included some of the greatest choral music ever written, including works by John Rutter, Pachelbel, and many other great composers.

That classical influence really had an effect on me: it was as if I was hearing something that was so much greater than my abilities to perform, but at the same time, inspired me to try. The challenge of performing a beautiful aria was unlike anything else I'd ever tried, and it was only a matter of time before I'd made up my mind that I wanted to be a singer in the classical mode. I focused on opera and put my heart and soul into learning that very demanding and exacting discipline.

It was a commitment that took up most of my time and energy, with not a lot left over for a social life. I had good friends in high school who were guys, but the relationships never got beyond the buddy stage. I had a very good reason for not taking dating too seriously. During my freshman year of high school my parents had made a deal with me: if I would keep away from drugs and alcohol and save sex for marriage, they promised to send me anywhere I wanted to go for my senior trip. Of course, since I'd decided on my own to stick to my Christian principles, my end of the arrangement wasn't hard to keep, and as a reward, I took a grand tour of Europe after graduation. I went with two other friends who, after they had heard about my parents' proposition, made the same deal with their parents, and we traveled through Holland, Germany, Switzerland, Austria, Italy, France, and England in high style.

Back home, I turned my attention to the next chapter of my life—higher education in hopes of finding a career as a classically trained singer. It was also when I got my first real taste of independence, after my family moved again, this time to Easton, Pennsylvania, where my father had been transferred by his company.

I went with them initially, but it was a very hard transition to make. I was about to graduate, and the thought of not being able to receive my diploma at the high school where I had earned it was difficult to imagine. Pennsylvania might as well have been the dark side of the moon as far as I was concerned, and my parents quickly saw that I needed more time to say good-bye to the life I had built in Norman. They agreed to let me return and live with some close family friends until school was over.

All in all, my senior year was more than a little traumatic for me, with my family moving and all the pressures of picking out a college. The prospect of the upcoming senior prom didn't help my stress level either. Although I didn't have a date, I decided to go anyway, along with a few other stag friends who just wanted to have a good time and commemorate the end of our high school years.

Usually, for any big event, my mom was around to help me get ready, which included giving my dark hair a few blond highlights. Of course she was hundreds of miles away in Pennsylvania, so I recruited a friend of hers who had gone to beauty school to help with my hair.

Well, I don't know if that sweet woman flunked all her classes or what, but by the time she finished with me, instead of a few light streaks I had a full head of shockingly blond hair. I didn't know what to do, but I finally decided not to let my new color ruin the night. So I went anyway, and believe me, I turned more heads than the prom queen.

It was strange being away from the love and support of my family, but it was also a great preparation for the next stage of my life, which came into focus with the news that I had received a scholarship to study vocal performance in the music program at Ouachita Baptist University.

I'd pretty much gotten used to moving around by that time, but there was something very special about having my family around me one more time as I got set to embark on this new life.

My whole family drove to Arkansas to help me get settled into my dorm room, and as the afternoon shadows lengthened and it got time for them to head back, I think we all felt like we'd come to a crossroads in the history of our little family.

My dad cried that day as the reality of leaving his first child so far away got closer and closer. Before I knew it, we were all crying, standing out there in the parking lot and praying for God's goodness and protection to follow us in all the days to come. It was a sad, sweet moment and a memory I'll always carry in my heart.

But I really didn't have much time to sit around and mope. The routine at Ouachita started off with a bang, and I soon realized that, however talented I thought I might be musically, I still had a very long way to go.

When it comes to music I guess I've always been something of a perfectionist. I've never really liked hearing my own voice on tape, because I have a tendency to second-guess my performance every time, realizing what I could have done better and wincing at all the little glitches that no one else even notices. And believe me, the tedious process of recording an album sometimes makes me feel like I've picked the wrong profession.

If my early days at Ouachita made me realize that the perfection I was seeking was all but unattainable, they also helped me to see that I still had room to grow. While I loved opera and sacred music, there were also other forms of musical expression that were just waiting to be tried, and that were tremendously exciting to me, such as show tunes, theater, and pop music.

It was also a time of real encouragement, as I developed my vocal gift and began to see my creative horizons expand. A high point was when I went out for an audition for the Metropolitan Opera Competition, which attracted some of the greatest singers in the country. The contest is held each year in different U.S. cities, with the winner from each region going on to the finals. The closest city to me was Little Rock, and I had the distinct privilege, at twenty years old, of being one of the youngest people to compete. While I didn't win, some of the judges had encouraging things to say about my performance afterward.

All in all, it was a great experience, and I felt good about the effort I had made. Not winning wasn't too disappointing, considering I was nowhere close to the caliber of the singers involved, and it was encouraging to realize that my repertoire was comparable to theirs. They were in their prime and it was a real inspiration to know that I could compete with them at that stage of my career and still hold my own. Who knew what tomorrow might bring?

When I was up onstage doing a recital it was a challenge for me to put myself into the character musically and lyrically, especially if it was in another language. I tried my best to put across all the emotion I felt when I listened to Leontyne Price or Joan Sutherland or some of the other great opera singers of our time. When I could get even a little of that feeling across, it gave me a great sense of accomplishment.

But even at the height of my grand dreams of being the youngest diva ever to grace the stage, I knew that there was more to singing than just the applause and encores. I'd heard that the world of opera is intensely competitive and could really be cutthroat and full of backbiting and jealousy. I just didn't think I could take it all that seriously. While the music meant a lot to me, I wasn't going to let it control my life. I was in college, on my own for the first time, and I wanted to have some fun.

So I made it my business to go out for all kinds of other activities that might challenge me and help me to grow. Although throughout college I performed in a lot of different variety shows, there was one that I was consistently involved with from my freshman year on. It was called the Ouachitones, and as you know, that was where the seeds were planted that eventually blossomed into Point Of Grace.

Now, you might be asking yourself at this point what happened to my opera career. Well, as that first summer with the group drew to an end and I returned to

Ouachita I more than once felt God tapping me on the shoulder, saying, in that quiet and gentle way of His, "You know, I've got other plans for you."

When I talk about God tapping me on the shoulder, however, I hope I haven't given you the idea that He and I meet regularly for breakfast every Tuesday morning or something. The truth is, sometimes I don't hear from Him at all, even when I really think I need guidance or direction. Like anybody else, I've had my spiritual highs and lows, and I've come to accept that as part of my Christian life. You can't always stay up on the mountain and you're not always going to be down in the valley. Life is a journey.

There's still a part of me that would love to sing at the Met someday, and another part that believes God would like that as well. To that end, I've worked with an incredible vocal coach who, though he appreciates the music I do with Point Of Grace, constantly encourages me to keep my classical aspirations alive as well. I even have the chance to utilize some of my opera training during my solo segments of our live show, and it seems that audiences like it just as much as I do.

But there came a time when I had to choose between one direction or the other: was I going to stay with the group or try for an opera career? Thankfully, God was so gracious, and when the time came, after my final year at college, it was as if I were looking at a big green arrow flashing "go" and pointing me in the direction of Point Of Grace. For better or worse, that was where my future lay, and for me, it's a choice that's been validated every single day since then. I've been given such a wonderful opportunity, not just to utilize my talent, but also, I hope, to make an impact on the lives of others.

I could see that God was blessing people through our music, but what I couldn't see at the time was that He had other plans for us as well. I got my first inkling of our new responsibilities when friends stopped asking us how we were doing with our music and asked instead how we were doing with our ministry.

Ministry! What ministry? We were just four young women having the time of our lives. But we soon came to see that God had more in mind than just keeping us entertained. We had something to tell our audiences . . . something that could make all the difference in the world to their lives.

Like everything else about the creation of Point Of Grace, the message of sexual purity was a natural outgrowth of our lives. We've always tried to present ourselves just as we are, with none of the glitter and glitz that so often comes with being in the entertainment business. Long before we got together, we had all decided that we were going to save ourselves sexually for marriage, and from that individual commitment came a collective resolution to help other kids make the same choice.

It was something back in those Bible camps we used to talk a lot about one-on-one with kids who were facing the pressures of growing up in ways that we never had to. The world had changed so much, even from the time we'd been in high school, that I think there were moments when we doubted that what we were trying to say would get through to a new generation of seekers and searchers.

You'd be surprised how the truth remains truthful down through the ages. Young girls and guys responded to the idea of chastity with an enthusiasm and sincerity that was really inspiring, and as our musical appeal spread, so, too, did word about our message of abstinence and virginity. It wasn't too long before the two would come together and we could truly say that our music and our ministry were twin facets of the same job God has given us to do.

There's nothing more exciting than knowing your purpose in life and then going out and doing it. I had made my decision to save myself for my husband because that's what my faith teaches me, but it wasn't a lesson I was meant to keep to myself. In Point Of Grace, and even as an individual, I've had wonderful opportunities to spell out my convictions, whether it's onstage, delivering a little talk between songs, or through the work we do for an organization called Mercy Ministries, which provides homes and adoption services for unwed mothers. I've even been given the privilege of talking in public schools, and the response is always the same. Some kids smirk, some could care less, but there's always a few who take what you're saying to heart, and it's those few who always make it worthwhile.

So here I am, five years down the road as part of Point Of Grace, and I'm still looking forward with eager anticipation to what God will write in the next chapter of my life.

I'm hoping, of course, that the chapter will include

marriage and a family, but one thing I've learned from being the only single member of the group is that I have to live the life that God has given me today and be content with His will for me in the here and now. It's so important to live every day thankfully, understanding that God knows the desires of my heart. I realize that in this society women are really under pressure to get married and have children, but I'm a firm believer in blooming where you're planted.

And single life really can bring rich rewards, if you are ready to receive them. Being by myself gives me time to improve who I am and strengthen my connection with God. The bottom line is, although it sometimes gets lonely on your own, those are the very same times when you need to depend on and trust God. I'd rather bear up under a little solitude than rush into something just because I was desperate.

In the meantime I have a fun and fulfilling career and there's a part of me that hopes that it will just keep going forever, allowing us to sing the music that we love and hopefully bless people with our ministry. Along with my hopes that one day I'll find the right guy and settle down, I guess that dream of having roses thrown at my feet on the stage of an opera house is still alive, as well.

But whatever happens, I know, beyond a shadow of a doubt, that God is in control. He hasn't taken me this far to leave me in the lurch. He hasn't made promises that He doesn't intend to keep. And what's true for me is true for you as well. My prayer is that you'll see His plan and purpose in your life as clearly as I've seen it in mine.

HEATHER FLOYD

Heather Lynaye Floyd, 6 months.

Ouch! My first birthday, when I burned my hand on the candle.

My younger sister, Misti, and me.

I often spent my childhood in quiet prayer. (Actually, I'm picking my nose.)

The Floyds: my sister, Misti, my mom, Brenda, me, and my dad, Travis. (Times sure have changed!)

My parents and me.

At a surprise 16th birthday party for me and my friends Amy and Deana.

The glamorous life.
Point Of Grace on a road trip to Estes Park for the Christian Artist Seminar.

Happy 16th Birthday
Heather Amy and Deana

Point Of Grace at our
very first photo shoot.
(We ended up rejecting
every picture!)

With all our proud parents
at the Dove Awards,
in April 1994.

With my precious baby,
Darla, in September 1995.

GOD ONLY KNOWS

We've touched on a lot of subjects between these covers, tried to be as up-front and in touch as we could possibly be, letting you know just what we think and feel about issues that affect every one of us.

Now comes one of the most important topics of all, the one that we firmly believe puts everything else into perspective, provides the answers to life's biggest questions, and offers the solution to problems we could never hope to solve in the pages of a thousand books.

That topic, of course, is Almighty God. By now you must have figured out that our faith in God is the number one priority for us—up there ahead of our music, our careers, even our families. The reason for that is simple: we try to put God at the heart of all those things, to give them over to His care and let Him guide and direct the way we live, the words we say, and the promises we make.

We know for a fact that everyone who picks up this book is not going to believe the same things we do: that the Bible is the Word of God; that Jesus Christ is the Son of God; and that we all have the opportunity to be used by Him.

All we can say is that these simple truths have stood the test of time, and that in each person who takes them to heart, they make a change that lasts a lifetime. We're not here to preach, judge, or try to talk you into anything. All we ever want to do, in our songs, in our lives, and in this book, is to let you know what God has shown us, and do what we can to pass that on.

So that's what this chapter is all about. Sure, there are a lot of problems in the world today, tragedies too terrible for us to imagine, warnings too urgent to ignore. But the God that we're talking about—the God that gave His only son so that we might know His love—is about more than just taking care of the mess we find ourselves in. He's about peace and joy and abundant living.

Knowing God is about more than just knowing a bunch of rules and regulations. It's about having a friend and a father; a teacher and a partner . . . someone who wants you to enjoy your life to the fullest and make every day a unique experience.

This is the God we're talking about—alive and well in hearts overflowing with excitement and enthusiasm and anticipation for the great things He's still got planned for us. Some of you may already know what we're talking about. To the rest, we hope that some of the things we touch on in here will give you an inkling of just who that God is—and why we want to celebrate Him with every word we sing, speak . . . or write.

Q: How can I discover God's will for my life?

Terry: I believe you're always discovering it. It's not like suddenly you know everything you need to know to figure out life totally. God reveals His plans a little bit at a time, giving you more as you grow. The happiness and contentment you feel within yourself is a good sign that you're living according to His plan. The Bible says that God is going to give you the desires of your heart, and even though we can't always be completely happy, if overall you've got contentment in your life, then that's a sign of His blessing.

For me, there are aspects of what we do in this group that make me unhappy, but I can generally say, "I feel settled. I feel like this is where I'm supposed to be and what I'm supposed to be doing."

Heather: Unless you spend time with God in a daily relationship, how are you supposed to know what to do from day to day? It's a relationship that you have to develop, to work on like any other one. Taking time to be with Him is the best way that you're going to know His will.

Q: More than anything I want to serve God. How can I best do that?

Shelley: It's in the little things of life. Some people are called to preach to the multitude. Others are called to go down to the local nursing home. There are so many ways to serve, and in the end, it goes back to finding your gift, what makes you happy. God's not going to give you a job that you hate.

Denise: When people say they really want to serve God, they need to check their motives, because the more you serve, the more you suffer. I truly believe that: the more you're going to say "yes" to God, the more you're going to say "no" to yourself. Yet, if we really give of ourselves and expect nothing in return, we can find a real sense of joy and purpose.

Q: Sometimes I wonder if God hears my prayers. How can I be sure?

Shelley: It's normal to wonder if God hears you. I think that there's always a response, but it just may not be what we want to hear, or when we want to hear it. If we know how to listen, sometimes even His silence is a response. We have to have faith that He is listening, and that He knows what we need, even if we sometimes don't.

I think we get confused sometimes. We think we want what God wants, but sometimes it's just our desires. He promises us ultimate happiness and He means it. But He knows what's best for us. We have to ask ourselves: is the desire of my heart something selfish or wrong? Then He's probably not going to let me have it.

Denise: It's not always going to be a clear voice that you're going to hear. Rarely in my life have I been totally sure that it was Him who I was hearing. It happened probably for the first time in my life about a month ago.

I was on an airplane by myself, coming home from Houston, Texas, praying for peace in my life because just then I was feeling a lot of turmoil. I was reading the Bible when all of a sudden I felt a total peace, a total security. I knew it wasn't just wishful thinking. It was real.

But that rarely happens to me, where I feel the holy presence of God. I think that when you're at a point of need in your life is when He comes to you in that way.

Terry: God says in the Bible that if His people who are called by His name will humble themselves and pray, then He will hear their voice. It's something you have to accept on faith. We ask ourselves, "Is He really hearing me? Why don't I feel His presence?" But even if you don't feel like anything's happening, God says He hears our prayers, that He is listening. And I'm going to choose to believe that, even if it doesn't always seem like it.

Q: Sometimes being a Christian is so hard. Why?

Terry: Sometimes being a Christian means going against the grain of people around us. It's hard to live one way when everyone else is living another. It's a battle to do what's right, and the opposition comes from both inside and outside us.

No real commitment is easy. When you ask God to forgive your sin, He will, but then you also have to do a complete turnaround and head the other way. That's not always easy and sometimes you're almost going to fail. But that's also when you get the strength that comes only by His grace, which gives you the will to keep going.

When I think about people reading this book it scares me that we're going to be misunderstood. We know that people who aren't necessarily Christians are going to read it. And we hope that they won't be so offended or turned off by what we have to say. But rather than just reading our words, if they really want to know who Point Of Grace is, look first at what we believe.

Heather: I know some people might say, "You guys are prudes. You're condemning. You're judgmental." But we can't live our lives seeking the approval of others. We have to do what we know is right and speak what we know is the truth if people ask.

Shelley: When it's hard to be a Christian is when you want the approval of other people. You can't always have that and still stick to your guns. You want your friends to think you're cool. You want people to think that you're normal. But they're not going to, so you can't change just to get that approval.

Denise: A lot of the issues we've talked about are sensitive, and any time you start getting into areas of strong beliefs and opinions, you're going to get resistance. God promises that being a Christian isn't always going to be a walk in the park.

We might be stepping on people's toes when we say we don't believe in having sex before marriage or that we don't believe in abortion. But I also think that people can be convicted by what we say, and that's why they put up their defenses. Our faith is an unapologetic statement. We say what we believe. Period.

Q: How does Mercy Ministries of America help girls facing an unplanned pregnancy?

Point Of Grace: We're so excited about our involvement with Mercy Ministries. There are so many girls out there who feel that abortion is their only option. We don't think that it's a quick and easy answer. But as Christians, it's not enough for us to say it's wrong; we have to put our money where our mouth is and give these girls a *real* option. Mercy Ministries provides free care, Christian counseling, adoption services, and practical teaching so that young mothers will know how to care for their babies should they elect to keep them instead of placing them up for adoption.

Q: When I try to share my faith, people turn away. Should I stop?

Shelley: No, but I think it's really important that you get to be somebody's friend first before you try to tell them what you believe. Even though you know what you're saying is the right thing and that the truth will set them free, you have to get into their life to a deeper extent before you can share in a way such that they can really hear you. Otherwise, it's going to be a complete turnoff. You just have to be careful.

Denise: You know, no one can save another person. It's not our responsibility; it's God's. Our responsibility is to live around those people in a way that sets an example and to share with them what's in our heart. Then God can reap what we sow. I think it's really important to be a friend and to show them that you love them unconditionally. Then, whether they accept what you believe or not, you've done your job. Five years later, when you're not even around, it might all finally sink in.

Q: Sometimes I don't understand the Bible. Am I dumb?

Heather: Not unless I'm dumb, too. There's so much I don't understand in the Bible. I think a lot of times it speaks to people in different ways. Some Scripture may say something clearly to one person and be a mystery to someone else. That's why it's so unique. It's a book that was written thousands and thousands of years ago and it is still reaching all sorts of different people today.

Terry: I wouldn't tell somebody who wants to get into the Bible to just start at Genesis and keep reading. Even though there's so much that's relevant there, you should start with the basics like the Psalms or Proverbs, or start with the New Testament.

Denise: There's all sorts of great translations, too. A lot of people grew up in really strict religious traditions where you only read one version of the Bible. But I find I get a lot out of comparing the translations. I have a *Living Bible* and *The Message,* which are great versions and make it a lot easier for me to work on those parts that I really don't get.

But no matter what version you have you've got to really get into it—study it every day. If there's a verse that speaks to you, get some background on who wrote it and what it was written for.

Shelley: Don't be discouraged if you're not a scholar the first time you open it. There's so much that I still don't understand. I come across a verse and say to myself, "What is God trying to tell me?" But it's so inspiring that people are still seeking truth there. The Bible is timeless. It's new for every generation.

Q: How can I best support my church?

Terry: A big part of being in any church is staying involved. You can't just go on Sunday morning to get yourself blessed. You've got to give something back. Be part of a leadership group or the youth group. Go on ski trips and other church events and get into a Bible study. Take advantage of what's being offered.

Heather: I think contributing regularly to your church is very important, too. You need to get into the habit of giving back part of what God's given to you. When you do it willingly and joyfully, there's something that just feels really right!

Denise: When I was growing up, my mom always took care of the family checkbook. She will say to this day that any month when she didn't give an offering something would happen that would cost the same amount of money, whether it was the car breaking down or something similar.

And when it didn't seem like there was going to be

enough money that month and she went ahead and tithed anyway, we always made it through. Somehow, the money always came. If we tithe, God blesses.

Q: My witnessing doesn't bear fruit. Why?

Shelley: Timing is everything. You may have planted a seed by what you've said, but it's up to someone else to bring in the harvest. Even though you may never know the result of what you do, God does. So, you may not think you're bearing much fruit but you just have to keep on trying.

Q: Should I be friends only with other Christians?

Terry: Of course not. We should be open to all friendships. God loves all people; we should too.

Heather: I think it's important, if you're a Christian, that you date a person whose beliefs and morals are the same as yours, because your beliefs will really make a difference in the direction of the relationship. It's good to be on the same wavelength. And I think your core friends, the ones who you spend a lot of time with and confide to, need to believe in what you believe, too. Ultimately, that's what draws you together as friends.

Denise: If you're asking advice from your friends, it's important to know their values. Don't get counsel from someone whose standards are lower than yours, because it's always easier to be brought down to someone else's level than for you to bring them up to yours.

Q: Does God have a mate picked out for me?

Heather: I sure hope so! But there are some people who God intends to be single. We all know that His plan is for our life to be abundant in goodness and many blessings. But does that mean that we're supposed to marry one particular person in one particular town? It just depends on how involved you think God is in those details.

Shelley: People who say that God has a plan for your life are right, but I honestly don't know if that includes one specific person you're supposed to marry.

It's wonderful and romantic to think that fate will bring you together with a special person. But I also think there are choices you make in your life. If I wasn't in Point Of Grace, I could have easily gone to graduate school and maybe met somebody there and gotten married. It's kind of a mystery and I'm not sure any of us can unravel it.

Terry: I think God plans your future spouse. I believe that for me the only man I could have ever been with is Chris. God knew every part of Chris and me and how we would fit together. We aren't perfect, and sometimes opposites attract, but I believe we were meant to be.

Q: Is divorce a sin?

Denise: While in the Bible It says God hates divorce, it's important for kids to know that, though it isn't good for parents to split up, God doesn't hate them. He loves them. These are situations that happen in real life and God can forgive and heal.

Terry: I once saw a program where they interviewed young kids from divorced families, and almost every one of them felt it was somehow their fault. They wanted to know, "Did I do something bad that made you leave?" They were searching for a reason for what happened. Parents really need to explain that it's not their kids' fault, and kids need to hear that from their parents. They may have a lot of questions and maybe a lot of bitterness, but they may not know how to talk about it and bring it out in the open. Some parents, when they get divorced, just withdraw into themselves. They're so hurt, and a child feels like they just can't win in that situation. They're completely on their own. They need to know that their life is not over.

Q: Why do bad things happen to good people?

Shelley: Let's face it, some questions are just never going to be fully answered in this life. One thing that's important to remember, however, is that God makes rules to live by and people see them as boundaries to keep them from having fun. The truth is, those rules are there to protect us.

The Bible has dozens of commands and standards that are like God's umbrella: when you put up an umbrella it shields you from the rain, but if you choose to move out from under the umbrella you're bound to get wet.

A lot of people try to blame God for tragedies that happen, but sometimes we need to look to ourselves and ask, "Have I moved out from under the rules?"

Heather: There's a great story in the Bible about Abraham and Sarah. Sarah couldn't have children, so she told Abraham, "I want you to have sex with my servant Hagar. She'll have your child and we'll raise it as our own." So Abraham and Hagar had Ishmael.

Later, Sarah became pregnant and got jealous; she was afraid that Ishmael was going to get Abraham's inheritance. So she drove Hagar and her son into the desert, trying to hide the consequence of the sin she had brought about.

But it was God, in His tender mercies, who saved Ishmael and said to Hagar, "I'm going to take care of this."

It's wonderful to see God working beyond the circumstances man creates by taking this little boy and making him a father of many nations. He was born in sin, but God had mercy on him like He has mercy on all of us, even though we can't see past the situation sometimes.

Denise: No matter what happens in your life, God is faithful. A good example of that is the great Christian writer C. S. Lewis, a man who had experienced a lot of tragedy. He went from being a Christian to being an atheist and then back around to being a Christian again. His faith was really tested, and in the end all that this brilliant man could say was, "Out of all these things

I've investigated, only Christianity proved true." To me, that's a real inspiration.

Q: Does God have a plan for my life?

Heather: God does have a plan for our lives. There's no question about it. Finding out what it is comes from seeking him, praying, and reading the Bible. I don't want to overspiritualize it, but God's will for us is very real. We've all four grown up in a Christian environment and feel very blessed to have that foundation. It's helped us feel secure.

I remember making sure that I read my Bible every day when I was in junior high school. No, I didn't always know exactly what was in store, but we all need to walk by faith and take life as it comes.

I don't think you'd want to know long-term what the plan for your life is. I know I'd rather be surprised.

Terry: Your life may take a totally unexpected turn when you're fifty. For instance, when my parents got married they weren't Christians, and now they work with a ministry for prisoners, just because of the experience my dad went through. There's no way in the world they would have ever known what they'd be doing now. God just does a flip-flop sometimes.

Shelley: I heard a neat allegory once. You're in a dark forest and you can't see where you're going. You have a flashlight, but the beam only takes you one step at a time. When I made a decision in junior high to save sex for marriage, little did I know that I would get to stand on a platform and speak about that decision. Just take a step at a time, trusting and believing that God has the path laid out.

Denise: It's probably good that we don't know. I know I can handle only one little piece of life at a time. I might want to change something and that's not up to me, that's up to God. The only decision I need to make is the one that's right in front of me, the choice at hand.

Q: Is the devil real?

Heather: Yes, and he's lurking to destroy us. But at the same time I don't think we should be looking under our beds for Satan. Some people see a devil on every tree branch and one on your shoulder. I think that demonic forces are real and we need to be aware of them, but at the same time fear can't control our lives.

There's certainly spiritual warfare all around us. The Bible tells us that, but you can also see it with your own eyes—the battle between good and evil that happens every day. I know that I've felt the presence of evil, very definitely, even inside myself. Just the other day I was driving down the road in a bad mood and got caught in traffic and I kept thinking these awful thoughts. I was getting mad, screaming in the car, and I suddenly thought, "You know what? I feel really evil right now." At times like those, I have to slow down and pray for forgiveness and patience.

Shelley: We have to be careful not to overspiritualize things. I see people do that all the time. Whenever something bad happens, even if they can't find a parking place, it's Satan trying to frustrate them.

But when you're down or things go wrong in your life, Satan can use that to plant doubts in your head: "Why is God allowing this? Why would God allow somebody that He loves to suffer?" Satan wants to destroy our inner beings because that's the part that matters the most—our spirits.

Terry: I think even with us, as Point Of Grace, we've seen that when the very best things are happening for us, something comes along to try and snatch it away.

For instance, when we won the Dove Award for the first time, everything was supposed to be great. That's exactly when the devil said, "Hey, they've had a real victory. Now's the time to pull them down!" And he began tearing at our relationships with each other. We were making our album and, at the same time, as a group we had to struggle more than ever to keep ourselves together. That was the devil, wanting to ruin the chance that people's lives might change because of our music. I think he didn't want us to record the actual words to some of our songs.

Denise: The devil goes after relationships and he also attacks our confidence and trust in God. In this group, he wants us to believe that we don't have what it takes to be in this position, that we can't deal with success. And that's a lie that we have to recognize and reject.

Q: How can I be a joyous Christian?

Heather: I think a great symbol of what Christianity

is all about is when Jesus washed the disciples' feet with a towel. The real meaning of Christianity is not in the scepter of a king; it's in that towel. Yes, He is the King of Kings and Lord of Lords, yet He came to us as a servant. He was perfect, yet He washed the disciples' feet. So I think joy comes from being a servant.

Terry: We see that ideal of servanthood every day in our work. Because we're up onstage performing, people tend to think we're the special ones and that we should be thanked for showing up. But, to me, it's our crew that's really special. They work so hard, and no one really sees the effort they're putting forth. I think that's what servanthood is all about. Doing something without any expectation of reward.

You should never get so used to people serving you that you forget to serve them. When others try to make you comfortable and happy, you can start getting used to that, and then you're heading for trouble. That's what happens with kids and parents sometimes. The children expect the parents to provide everything, and when they don't get what they want, they think they're being deprived. So often kids think their parents are trying to run their lives, but I can't think of a better example of servanthood than what parents do for their children.

Shelley: When you're truly serving, there's a sacrifice involved. For me that sacrifice comes after the concert when we stand out in the lobby and talk to people and sign autographs. There's always that one last person in line and you're so tired you don't want to talk to any-body else. But that kid is tugging on your shirt and really wants a piece of your time and wants you to listen to them—really listen to them and look them in the eye. That's where the sacrifice begins, and that's where serving someone really has meaning. And if I can do that, I get a greater reward than the kid.

It's easy to get up onstage. Let's be honest: we can fake our way through a whole concert and nobody would ever know. We can smile and put on a show. But when we're talking to people face-to-face is when you can tell. That's when it really counts.

Denise: Certainly the hardest part of serving is being a servant to my friends and my husband and my family. You don't mean to, but sometimes it's so easy to take the ones you love for granted. When I get home after being on the road, there's nothing I'd like better than just to go to bed and not think about anything, but that's the only time I have to spend with Stu. It's in moments like that when I realize that the call we have to be of service to one another starts at home.

MEET SHELLEY PHILLIPS

Name: Shelley Lynn Phillips
Birthday: May 1, 1969
Birthplace: Belleville, Illinois
Education: Bachelor of Music, vocal performance,
  Ouachita Baptist University
Favorite Color: Green
Favorite Food: Chips, salsa, and anything unhealthy
Favorite Clothing Designer: Donna Karan
Favorite Book: *The Firm* by John Grisham
Favorite Scripture: Romans 8:28
Favorite Actors: Tom Hanks, Meg Ryan
Favorite Vocalist: Vince Gill
Favorite Musical Style: Country (and all my
  solos on our records)
Favorite Movie: *Miracle on 34th Street*
Favorite TV Show: *Friends*
Favorite Cosmetics: MAC makeup
Favorite Perfume: Mackie
Favorite Holiday: Christmas
Favorite Animal: Cute little dogs

Favorite Waste of Time: Lying around watching TV and eating, or walking around the mall

Most Memorable Experience: Giving a speech at the Dove Awards and feeling so proud and happy for all that we had accomplished

Most Embarrassing Experience: When my button popped off my jacket during a concert and the audience could see my bare stomach shining in the spotlight

Happiest Memory: Christmas when I was eight. I got a toy stove, sink, and refrigerator. I loved it!

Saddest Memory: Hearing "Taps" at my grandfather's funeral in 1989

Most Treasured Possession: My dad, mom, sister, and fiancé

Best Personal Quality: My humor, good looks, striking personality, and overall humbleness

Worst Personal Quality: Too opinionated and loud

Proudest Accomplishment: The Dove Award for New Artist of the Year

Greatest Ambition: To be a wife and mother

Guilty Pleasure: Spending too much money on myself

Highest Ideal: To have a personal relationship with God

Some people say that they don't believe in miracles. And, if they're talking about Santa Claus, the Easter

Bunny, or a blind date with Tom Hanks, well, I guess they're entitled to their opinion.

But, for me, Shelley Phillips, there's no question that miracles are real . . . and they happen every day. What others call chance or coincidence, those little things that you can't exactly explain, I like to think of as the moments that define the direction of our lives . . . that, and what restaurants we eat at.

Just think about it: what if your mom or dad hadn't just happened to meet on a particular day in a particular place? What if the guy or girl next door who you ended up marrying had lived in another house across town? Or what if you'd never had Point Of Grace as an ideal role model for your life?

Just kidding, but you get the idea. The world is full of "what ifs," but for me, every "what if" has a "here's why" behind it, and the reason for all those twists of fate is simple: there's no such thing as accidents.

Everything, I believe, happens for a reason, and whether or not we ever discover that reason doesn't change the fact that our lives have a purpose, a point and a place to go. Every one of us has a part to play in God's "big picture," and each part fits, like the pieces of a puzzle, into every other piece. Our lives intersect, our paths cross, and we can all become miracles in someone else's life. Take me, for instance. I'm sure Heather, Terry, and Denise would all agree that I've been a miracle in their lives, ever since I let them become my backup singers and their careers finally took off.

But seriously, as part of Point Of Grace, I hear about

miracles happening every day. Traveling across the country we meet all kinds of people with all kinds of stories, and more often than not those stories are about troubled kids looking for answers, or parents with a problem child, or a young girl wondering about taking the next step with her boyfriend.

And sometimes they tell us about how they were helped through the hard times, found inspiration or comfort or even an answer from one of our songs that they heard on the radio, or some line from a lyric on the back of our albums, or even in the way a certain melody stayed with them through the day.

When we hear those simple stories, it makes us both humble and proud. It's a wonderful feeling when we realize that something we've done has had a positive impact on a total stranger, but we've also got to admit that, when you get right down to it, those miracles really don't have all that much to do with us. We were just in the right place at the right time, because that's the way God planned it.

But even understanding how God, sometimes without us knowing it, can reach out through our songs to touch a heart or answer a prayer, doesn't completely prove to me that miracles happen. The real proof is that four women came together to become Point Of Grace in the first place.

The fact that we found each other, that our voices blended in harmony, and that we found a common purpose to keep us together—that's the biggest miracle of all. I should know: it's a miracle that someone as smart and beautiful as I am could tolerate hanging around those other three.

But the truth is, miracles do happen, every day, and everywhere you look. And if they can happen for us, they can happen for you, too.

My particular story began on May 1, 1969, when I came into the world in Belleville, Illinois, a town near St. Louis. That's where my dad, Joe, was stationed on an air force base.

I really loved my hometown and have such fond memories of each and every one of the twenty days I spent there. You see, when I was still a baby, my dad was sent off to Korea, and my mom, Sharon, and I moved to Michigan, to the small Upper Peninsula town of Rudyard, where she was from and where she first met my dad.

He, in turn, had moved there when my grandfather, who was also in the military, was stationed on a base near Lake Superior. My mom and dad had been sweethearts all through high school and were married pretty soon after graduation.

While my dad was away, we lived with my grandparents, and my mom remembers that when she'd ask me, "Where's Daddy?" I'd toddle over and pick up his picture on the nightstand. When I was one, he came back from the war, and it wasn't long afterward that he packed us up and moved us down to Jacksonville, Arkansas, where his family roots were.

My parents were like two peas in a pod—round, green, and nutritious. Seriously, even though they

169

came from such different parts of the country, they have a lot in common. While my mom was born in the frigid North, she hardly fits that cold stereotype; she's one of the warmest and most sincere people I know. She reminds me a little of Denise in that way: she never wants to rock the boat and won't rest until she knows everyone is comfortable. She's so nice sometimes I want to tell her, "Stick up for yourself a little more, Mom!" But then I realize I might not get the benefit of her love and protection, so I keep it to myself.

I guess my dad fits the typical southern style a little closer. He's very easygoing and gentle, and has a sense of humor that's almost as off-the-wall as mine, with bad puns and practical jokes that he never hesitates to inflict on anyone within range. People say that I take after him a lot, with all my smart aleck remarks, which usually gets them a smart aleck remark right back. But for both of us, it's always just in fun. I've actually been told I used to look a lot like my dad, before I shaved my beard.

As far as I can tell, I'm sort of a mix of both of my parents. As I've gotten a little older, I've become more concerned with people's feelings and I'd never intentionally say something to hurt a person or make them uncomfortable . . . well, maybe just make them squirm a little once in a while. The truth is I really can't help saying just what I think, even if sometimes it's not what others want to hear. Hey, who said life was a popularity contest? Most of the time, though, I'm just trying my best to balance out the two sides of my personality.

It was in Jacksonville that my parents finally put

down roots and got about the business of raising a family. Anyway, that's where I have my first real memories of childhood, going to kindergarten at Ding Dong Campus, which I guess helps explain how I got this way.

Ding Dong Campus was the scene of many of my earliest triumphs and tragedies, the kind of things that seem like such a big deal when you're a kid and make such great memories when you're grown up and wishing your life were that simple again. Kindergarten was where I had my first crush on a boy, a freckle-faced heartthrob named Travis. But our romance never got off the ground, mainly because I couldn't quite pronounce his name: instead of "Travis" it always came out "Frabdus," which seemed to get him really mad. "You can't even say my name right!" my Romeo would yell.

One of my earliest childhood traumas also occurred in the hallowed halls of Ding Dong, and it's more than a little embarrassing to talk about it now. Of course, when did I ever let embarrassment get in the way of a good story?

Anyway, there was a big scandal in my kindergarten class when some junior juvenile delinquents took toilet paper rolls and threw them into the bowl, leaving a soggy, clogged-up mess behind. Now, I know you'll find this hard to believe, but I wasn't among those peewee vandals, and one afternoon when I was sitting on the toilet, I looked around and saw that the only paper available was one of those soaked rolls. I yelled to my teacher to bring some more, but she refused, stubbornly insisting that we kids had to learn a lesson about making mischief. So there I was, innocent as a lamb with a dirty bottom!

Well, I stayed on that toilet for an hour, sniffling and sobbing until my dad came to pick me up. When we got back home and I told him what happened, he got right on the phone and let that teacher have it while I sat at the kitchen table, smugly sucking on a grape Popsicle.

I can still clearly remember my graduation from Ding Dong Campus—wearing those little white caps and gowns—and maybe that's because I was the speaker and recited a poem in front of all the parents. Even at five I was hogging the stage. In fact, when I think back on myself during those early years, I can still see a spunky little kid who was always ready to go for it— whatever "it" might be. For example, my best friend, Alice, and I would spend every recess out on the playground with our little shovels playing in the dirt. Were we making mud pies? Not exactly. We were digging for the devil, absolutely convinced that if we kept at it, we'd find a big red man with a tail, horns, and pitchfork at the bottom of our hole. And when we did, were we ever going to give him a piece of our minds!

Because he had served as a medic, when my dad got out of the air force he went on to the University of Central Arkansas to get a degree in nursing. My mom supported us during that time, putting him through school by working as a secretary for the federal government.

We lived in a trailer for those early years, and even

to this day my dad claims he'd be a rich man if we'd only stayed in that "mobile mansion," as he calls it, instead of buying a real house, with a real mortgage. Sometimes I joke with the girls and tell them I was a double-wide darling, but I remember having the time of my life in that little trailer park.

Our cramped mobile home was my whole world growing up, and it had its own share of dark crannies and mysterious corners, including my parents' bedroom, laid out at one end. It had come decorated with red velvet curtains and a bedspread trimmed in black tassels. With dim lights shining under yellow shades, the whole place had a strange and spooky air to me, and I remember thinking that for sure there was a fortune-telling gypsy lurking back there somewhere.

Another one of my earliest memories took place on Easter Sunday when I was playing with my cousin Bruce, my dad's sister's son, who lived two trailers down from us and was my best friend growing up. He was a year younger than me, and we were inseparable as youngsters. Bruce would wait patiently all day for me to get back from kindergarten. Even then I guess I was driving boys simply crazy . . . even though it was just my cousin.

Anyway, on this particular Easter, Brucie and I went out into the front yard, where the Easter Bunny, or a reasonable facsimile, had drawn big arrows in the dirt pointing to our respective sides of the yard, where a banquet of Easter candy was waiting for us. Before that day was over, I had collected an entire plastic garbage bag full of the stuff.

I was always a little bossy, and before I even knew I could sing, I would force little Bruce and my other cousin, Paul, to be my backup singers. I'd stand on my stage (a toybox) with my microphone (a hairbrush) and my band (an LP of "Sigmund and the Seamonsters"), and sing at the top of my lungs, while Bruce and Paul were forced to sing backup from under the bed. That's right—I'd force them right under there. I mean, after all, *I* was the star.

I guess you could say that, all in all, growing up was great for me, with fun and good times filling my little world. I had my parents pretty much to myself until I was eight, which was when my sister, Robyn, was born. Because we were so far apart in age, we weren't really that close for the first years together. I remember trying to get her to sing with me when we were young, but she never seemed that interested in just being my backup vocalist. Funny, but I have the same problem now with Denise, Heather, and Terry.

It's only as we got older that Robyn and I got to know each other better, and I'm very thankful for that. I'll always be grateful to her for what she's taught me about sharing and communicating with other women. Believe me, it's come in pretty handy in my career.

I can't remember a time when I didn't feel safe, secure, and loved. My dad went to work as a nurse, and I even got used to the teasing I'd get at school, when the kids asked me whether he wore a dress. My parents were always there for me, even though I can remember times when my dad was studying hard to get his degree and I would beg him unmercifully to come out to the playground and push me on the swings, like the other dads did. Lots of times he just couldn't get away, and it wasn't until I got older that I realized how guilty I must have made him feel. I could really be a little terror if I put my mind to it.

Church was a part of the contented picture of my childhood from the very beginning, but after spending time with Denise, Terry, and Heather, I know that my early encounters with God were a lot different from theirs. I said a while back that Point Of Grace was one group made up of four very different individuals, and I think our experiences in church prove the point.

First of all, the other three all came from strong Baptist backgrounds, while I was raised in a Lutheran church. Now, anyone who knows those two denominations will tell you they can be as different as night and day. Is one holier than the other, with a bigger blessing or a direct line to heaven? I don't think so, and while I'm sure there are those who might disagree, I don't believe any single church has an exclusive claim on God's truth. Anyway, that's my opinion, and as you've probably guessed, I've got opinions for every occasion.

Anyway, while faith in God was very important for my parents, they kept it pretty much to themselves. While there was never any doubt, as I was growing up, that they believed in the Bible, it wasn't like we really talked about it all that much. In fact, I later found out that there was a time before I was born when my dad didn't spend much time in church. He'd come from a broken family and had a hard childhood, and I think there were a lot of things he had to work out with God.

When I first started singing as a child, I joined a youth group choir in a church down the street in Little Rock, which was a true-blue Baptist congregation. Some of the kids there asked me if I'd ever had a "born-again experience": in other words, had I ever walked down the aisle, said the sinner's prayer, and accepted Jesus as my personal Lord and savior?

Well, in the Lutheran church they have what's called confirmation, which is when you're twelve and you go through some very extensive classes that culminate in a public acknowledgment of Christ as Lord, spoken in front of the church.

But when they talked about "being saved" I knew that wasn't what they meant. The truth was, I never heard that phrase growing up, and when I was finally confronted with it, it really made me wonder. I spent a lot of time searching my heart and thinking back on my awareness of God and His presence in my life. It's like that old saying: if I were arrested for being a Christian, would there be enough evidence to convict me? To tell the truth, I wasn't sure that the handcuffs wouldn't just slip right off.

That may sound funny coming from a contemporary Christian singer who gets up onstage every night and sings and talks about God. But for me, it was a very serious issue. The doubt I had was really starting to trouble me.

Well, it all got settled the summer after my freshman year in high school. I'd been singing at the Baptist church for a while, and when I was invited to a summer camp over vacation, I didn't think twice about accepting. After all, there'd be boys, free food, and no one to answer to for a whole week. There would also be lots of singing, and as my interest in music grew I was beginning to find out that my family's Lutheran church didn't offer as many musical opportunities. There weren't a lot of contemporary selections in the service, and the congregation was very small. Although one of my best friends was the daughter of our pastor and we used to go to Sandi Patty concerts together, our church didn't have a dynamic youth choir like the Baptists'.

That summer, in fact, became a time when I developed a real love for Christian music. Before then, I'd had my ear glued to Top 40 radio, and like most kids, had my personal favorites: Michael Jackson, the Bee Gees, and Chicago were at the top of my list back then. I still remember standing in front of my mirror with a hairbrush for a microphone and singing "Beat It" at the top of my lungs.

But contemporary Christian music, with its positive messages that uplifted audiences instead of getting them all hot and bothered, held a whole different attraction for me. I could really get behind the lyrics, and even though I wasn't always sure about what some of the catch phrases meant, it was the spirit that moved me.

Anyway, one weekend at that camp, a speaker talked about God in a way I'd never heard, bringing biblical principles into everyday situations. At the end of the session, he invited anyone who wanted to dedicate their life to Jesus to walk down the aisle where some camp counselors would be waiting to pray with them.

Well, I was the first one out of my seat, but it wasn't because I had some burning spiritual desire, at least not at that moment. More than anything I was curious as to what all this "born-again" talk was really about and also, to be truthful, a little bit afraid that maybe I wasn't automatically going to heaven after all.

When I got down to the altar, one of the counselors took me aside and started asking me questions. I answered them as best as I could, wondering all the while what was going to happen next. Yes, I had been baptized when I was little; no, I don't ever remember a time when I didn't believe in God; yes, I tried to live my life according to the words of the Bible.

It was all getting a little confusing and then she asked me a question that stopped me cold: "How did I know that God was real?" For the first time I really had to examine my faith: was it something handed down to me by my mom and dad? Was it because I was scared of going to hell? Was it a deep-rooted conviction or just something I had always assumed was right?

All this was going through my head, and I guess the counselor could see that I was having a hard time. She got up and brought over the speaker, and together, the two of them talked to me. It wasn't like an interrogation: I felt their genuine concern and a desire to understand that was as real as my own.

Over the next half hour I had a real heart-to-heart with them as they asked me in detail about my upbringing and what I had been taught at home and in church. As the conversation continued, a slow realization began to dawn on me: my life really had been touched by God—not in some dramatic, all-in-a-moment event—but through the whole course of my childhood.

I guess that realization must have shown on my face because just then the speaker hugged me and smiled and said, "I don't think you've got anything to worry about." When I heard that, I let out a long sigh of relief. Maybe I didn't know all the terminology about being born-again or baptized in the Spirit, but I knew God loved me and that I loved Him and that was good enough for me.

While I may not have been exactly sure what being a Christian meant, I had no doubt about what being a singer was all about. It seems to me that ever since I was a little girl, I've had the need to express myself, loud and clear, to get noticed, or, let's face it, just plain grab the attention. Maybe all kids are like that, wanting to yell "Look at me!" but as I got older the feeling didn't go away. In fact, it got stronger.

Fortunately, I found an outlet for that urge, one that gave me a way to channel some of that energy in a creative direction. Even though I'd always been drawn to music—whether it was on the radio or in the church—I hadn't yet discovered whether I had any talent of my own.

That discovery came in the seventh grade with a great music teacher who really inspired all of us with her dedication and vision. It had been her idea to form the choir, since our school had never had one before. I remember how thrilled I was when she selected me as part of the group that she wanted to try out for the All-Region Choir.

Well, I didn't make it to the finals that year, but it was close, and the encouragement I got to keep on singing was all I really needed. The next year I ranked even higher, and I think that's when I first seriously considered that maybe I really did have some ability.

When the choir teacher gave me a solo for a big concert, that possibility really blossomed. It was the first time I'd ever sung in front of a real audience, and there I was, belting out Olivia Newton John's "I Honestly Love You" in my goofy-looking choir outfit. I loved it. From then on, I signed up for every singing opportunity that came along, and pretty soon I was a part of not only the All-Region but also the All-State Choir, the youth choir at the local Baptist church, and the adult choir for my Lutheran congregation.

Whatever dreams of stardom I might have had, however, were brought right back down to earth by the day-to-day realities of high school and the trials of teenage life. The school I went to was very small, about 120 kids in my class, and had earned the nickname of "Redneck Tech" for its down-home flavor. Our campus was way out in the boonies with a lot of country kids, and while it was rumored that we had spittoons in the hallways, I never actually saw one.

What I did see a lot of was pickup trucks and gun racks, with Hank Williams Jr. cassettes in the tape player and a six-pack of beer under the seat. No self-respecting teenager would be caught without those vital accessories, but for me, trying to make an impression just took too much time and energy. I never disapproved of the kids who liked to party every weekend, but I never joined in either.

In fact, I really had only one close friend during that time. Her name was Maria and we pretty much stuck to ourselves. In fact, we both volunteered to work the cash registers in the cafeteria one year, which I guess made us look like hopeless nerds, but what did we care? We got a free lunch out of the deal—chicken nuggets, french fries, and a Snickers bar—which I'd somehow forgotten to tell my mom about. She kept faithfully forking over lunch money every day until Maria let the cat out of the bag and told her about our free lunches. Thanks, pal.

Singing had really become the center of my life, and as I entered my senior year I began to lay out plans for a career in music: get a master's degree in voice performance and teach music at the university level.

A big step toward realizing that goal came when I got a music scholarship to Ouachita Baptist University. Going to college was a chance for me to find out about myself: who I was, who I wanted to be, and how to make it all happen. Though being a music major was a lot of hard work, my social calendar also started to fill up. People seemed to appreciate me more, or at least they laughed at more of my jokes, which I've always considered the truest mark of a person's intelligence, good taste, and discernment.

At Ouachita I kind of "clicked," and it wasn't long before what used to be considered my weird streak was coming in very handy. I joined a social club and started getting asked to emcee our various productions. It wasn't always as easy as it sounded. I discovered that though I had a gift for a good off-the-cuff one-liner, I often fell flat when trying to be funny on cue. My sense of humor was definitely of the spontaneous variety, so I had to work extra hard thinking up jokes beforehand to get laughs.

It was during my first year at Ouachita that I joined the Ouachitones and met Denise Masters (Jones to all of you, now), beginning a tried-and-true friendship that's lasted to this day. Denise was everything you could ask for in a friend: considerate, committed, and totally up-front. Best of all—she pretended to like me, which meant I was able to overlook her more glaring faults.

To make sure my education was really well rounded, I started taking classes in opera, where I got to meet one of Denise's Oakie girlfriends: Heather. I was also introduced to Terry, and we all got along great. Denise and I even shared a dorm room in our junior year.

We remained close friends even after I left the Ouachitones to join another singing group, the Praise Singers, a collection of four guys and four girls who traveled to other schools doing Christian concerts. I learned a lot by being in the Praise Singers: how to live on the road; how to give a good performance even when you're tired and homesick, and how to leave a lasting impression on people who you may only encounter one time. They were lessons I would have occasion to use a lot in the years to come, even though at the time I was absolutely sure I wanted to be a teacher once I graduated.

Of course, things don't always work out exactly the way we plan, no matter how sure we think we are. I remained with the Praise Singers through my senior year at school, and even auditioned for another group called Truth. By that time I was beginning to have some serious second thoughts. Teaching had always been my idea of a safe and secure career, but after four years at college, I'd encountered a lot of creative people who were willing to take risks to realize their dreams. My career choice was beginning to seem less like a true calling and more like a convenient choice.

Denise, of course, knew all about the decisions facing me, but even so, I'm sure she didn't have anything special in mind the night she told me about the trio she had formed with Heather and Terry.

As she laid out their plans to perform locally during summer vacation, it seemed like a great idea and a lot of fun, and all of a sudden I heard myself saying, "I'd love to sing with y'all!" I mean, it wasn't like I was making a lifetime commitment, or anything. They were just talking about one summer, a summer I'd probably be spending at home, anyway, worrying about my future.

I don't know what my parents must have thought

when I came home and told them I was going to travel with a singing group all summer. But if they had reservations, they kept them to themselves. Maybe they picked up on the excitement I was feeling, and once we actually started booking concert dates, maybe they started to see that there might be a future in it, too.

What that future was, however, I don't think any of us could have guessed. At first, our little quartet was nothing more than a lark; a way for us to do what we loved and maybe earn a little—and I mean a little!— money over the summer.

Everything we did was on a shoestring budget. For instance, when we were on the road, we had a rule that if we stopped at McDonald's, we could each get a regular hamburger with fries or a regular hamburger with a Coke; but never both fries *and* a Coke. Even though we really had to scrimp and save to make ends meet, I still remember those days as the most fun and adventurous of our career.

Once, on an Arkansas highway in the middle of the night, we got a flat tire. With no money to pay the tow truck driver, we offered to sing him a song for a ride to the nearest gas station. There we were, standing by the side of the road in the freezing night singing our hearts out to an audience of one!

Most of the time we slept in a van that we'd borrowed from the parents of Terry's future husband, Chris. Whenever we did allow ourselves a night in a motel, it seemed like an incredible luxury, even with all four of us squeezed in one room.

On other occasions, the churches where we performed offered to put us up, although it wasn't always in the best of accommodations. At one stop, they parceled us out to different families in the congregation, and I ended up at the house of a cat-loving old lady. The smell of that place was, to say the least, pungent, and with cat hair and Kitty Litter boxes everywhere, I didn't have much choice but to spend the night rolled up in my garment bag.

We did everything for ourselves back then, taking alphabetical turns driving the van and unloading our own equipment. I never really slept well when Terry was at the wheel, thanks to her habit of having a nice soothing cup of cocoa before her shift, instead of gulping back a Coke or a cup of coffee to stay awake. We had more than one near-death experience with her at the wheel.

More often than not, we also had to do all the work of setting up our equipment when we got to the show. I remember once hauling speakers up a flight of stairs in our high heels and stage clothes while a bunch of southern gentlemen looked on admiringly, commenting as we passed by, "Y'all are real strong ladies." Right after the performance, of course, we had to pack everything up again, and there was more than one night when we'd be unplugging the mikes and dragging off the speakers before the last note of our encore had faded.

Of course, if we didn't get off the stage on time we always had Denise's boyfriend, and future husband, Stu, around to move things along. Before we could hire a professional soundman, Stu used to run our equipment, which mostly consisted of flipping the On switch for our background music tapes. Well, if he thought we were talking too much or hogging the spotlight too long, He'd just cut off the juice, and that would be the end of the show.

As you can well imagine, we had our share of low points during those first years together. In fact, if you show us a map of the southern states, we could point out exactly where they were. One that will forever live in infamy was the Barnacle Inn in Myrtle Beach, Virginia, a motel so grungy that even the cockroaches had moved out. Myrtle Beach, of course, is a famous party spot for vacationing college kids and the old Barnacle looked like it hadn't been cleaned since spring break . . . of 1923.

Then there was that little town in South Texas that shall remain nameless where Heather and Terry were put up in the house of one of the church members. The trouble was, the place wasn't all that spacious, and the two of them spent the night in the living room on a rollout bed, with no air-conditioning and one itchy Mickey Mouse blanket between them. Even that wouldn't have been so bad, if it hadn't been for the teenage son who hung around ogling them half the night.

Another blot on our map of all-time lows would have to be this one small town in northern Arkansas, where we did a concert at the First Baptist Church. Now, when you're a Christian entertainer, there's many times when you perform for whatever money the church can get together, and the good folks at First Baptist assured us they'd make it worth our while.

Well, their idea of what our "while" was worth was a lot different from ours. We got an inkling of just what we were in for when we saw the accommodations they'd provided for us: the ramshackle home of an old lady who spent the entire evening canning blueberries. After a long night of traveling and performing all we wanted to do was relax in front of the TV, but when *Cheers,* one of our favorite shows, came on, that old lady stomped over to the set and switched it off with her blue-stained fingers, proclaiming that any program that took place in a bar was "of the devil."

The next morning we were all looking forward to the big breakfast the church said would be provided. Imagine our surprise when it arrived and turned out to be a paper bag full of Little Debbie snack cakes. Now, anyone who's been to this town knows that its one claim to fame is that it's the home of the Little Debbie factory, which meant those cakes were probably the cheapest you could buy around there, not counting chicken feed, which anyone will tell you just doesn't cut it for the most important meal of the day.

For every hard time, however, there were a dozen good times to make up for it. During those first years together, we worked hard to make Point Of Grace a reality, but when it came to the real career opportunities, those always seemed to happen without our even trying. At least, that's how I remember it. How else can you explain some of the "coincidences" that put four total unknowns in front of appreciative audiences night after night? Of course, they were mostly there to see me, but I've always tried to keep that from the other girls.

For instance, during our second year together, our publicity picture and tape made their way onto the desk of a talent organizer for one of the biggest Christian youth events in the country: the Youth Evangelism Conference in Texas. Something about our sound caught his ear, and almost before we knew it we found ourselves singing for twenty-four thousand kids.

Naturally, there were other youth pastors at the event, and we were quickly booked solid at camps and churches across the South. Eventually we ended up at the big Christian music showcase in Estes Park, Colorado, which is where we were first approached by Word Records about recording an album. The rest, as they say, is history.

Of course, it all didn't happen at once, and in the meantime, we had to keep plugging along, even when it wasn't so clear that the group could, or even should, hold together. People sometimes ask us about the dynamics within Point Of Grace—like who's friends with who and how we all get along. Well, it would be less than truthful if I said we greet each other every day with sunny smiles, but from my experience in being around other groups, it's really amazing how well we coexist.

Naturally, most of that is due to my proven leadership abilities. It wasn't long after we got together, in fact, that I earned the fond nickname of Boss Hogg, from the character in *Dukes of Hazard*. I guess I've always had a bossy streak in me, but it really got a workout in those early years. The funny thing was, every time I'd loudly announce where we were going, how we were getting there, and what we would do when we arrived, Heather and Denise would always jump to it, just because I sounded so sure of myself. Only later would they ask themselves why they'd been so quick to follow my lead. (Terry, on the other hand, pretty much ignored me, but then, there's always one bad apple in the bunch.)

As far as who is friends with who, while I can't think of three people I'd rather spend endless hours in a tour bus with, I'd also probably have to say that I know Denise the best, if only because we've been friends the longest. But when she got married and I moved into a condo with Heather and Terry, that's when I really started to find out more about them. I could tell you stories, but I'm far too much of a lady for that. Besides, they've got a few tales they could tell on me.

Of course, now that Terry's married and living in Little Rock, it's Heather that I've gotten to know the best. Ask the other girls and I'm sure you'll get different answers, but personally I think our relationships are healthy because we try hard to keep the lines of communication open and it's important that none of us gets more of the spotlight than the others. We always try to be honest about everything, and because we love and respect each other, we've learned how to make allowances, give each other space, and cut ourselves a little slack. Those are the constants that endure, through all the challenges and changes.

Actually, change itself is another constant in our lives. Just when we think we've got everything in line and under control, something comes along to keep us on our toes, moving us out of our comfort zones into untested new areas, both personally and professionally. I guess it's God's way of letting us really know who's boss.

One of the greatest changes that's happened in my life recently was my engagement earlier this year. Of course, the prospect of getting married, even to someone as wonderful as my fiancé, David, makes me wonder what the rest of my life is going to look like: mother and wife, singer and performer, or something in-between?

When I look at the adjustments Terry and Denise have had to make, I find myself wondering if I can keep all those balls in the air as well as they do. It's a question I guess will be answered after the honeymoon, but for right now, I'm just content to bask in the glow of finding someone as great, gorgeous, and gentlemanly as my future husband. He's the greatest thing that's happened to me since I first laid eyes on Frabdus.

David and I met about two years ago, when our paths first crossed in the Christian music business. He's a booking agent for the William Morris Agency, which means that he arranges concert dates for groups like Point Of Grace.

At first I thought he was really cute, but to be honest with you, at the time I was about thirty pounds overweight and not too happy with myself, so I couldn't imagine that anyone else would be, least of all a good-looking guy like David.

We kept bumping into each other off and on over the next several months, and during that time I lost a lot of weight and really got my act together. I had a few relationships before David finally asked me out two years later, so I didn't necessarily feel like it was the greatest miracle of all time. The truth was, we made a good couple, which Denise and the others kept pointing out so often that I started to believe it myself.

Whenever I heard stories about love at first sight or somebody seeing their future mate and knowing it immediately, I always scoffed. That sort of thing happened in romance novels, soap operas, and some of my more outrageous daydreams, but never in real life. Well, I'm here to tell you it's true. After a few dates with David, all I can say is that I knew that this was the guy I was meant to be with. I even felt a little bad about being so sure: I always thought you were supposed to overcome your doubts and second thoughts so that by the time you walk down the aisle there are no questions left. Well, for me there were no questions from almost the very beginning, except when, exactly, he was going to pop the question.

Even though I was expecting it—actually it was more like holding my breath for six solid months—when it finally happened it was a complete surprise, thanks to David's determination that I wouldn't guess what he was up to.

To make sure his plan came off perfectly, he put together an elaborate scheme that everyone in the group was in on. We were in Colorado Springs in February of last year doing a concert, and the night before we were scheduled to go back home I got a call from him. He was in Nashville, he told me, anxiously awaiting my return.

Actually, what everybody knew except yours truly was that he was just down the street from our hotel, making some very special arrangements for a surprise that would last me a lifetime.

After the concert, while we were signing autographs, Denise, in her best heartfelt tone of voice, told me a sad story about a teenage fan who needed some counseling backstage. She was acting very strange, but then again, it was Denise, so strangeness was something I'd pretty much come to expect.

Even so, as I followed her around to the rear of the stage, I heard a little voice in the back of my mind asking what she was up to. That voice got louder when I saw the big white limo with a red carpet rolled out in front, but even then I didn't catch on. I just assumed this troubled teen must be out on one fancy date.

It was just about then that David burst out of the limo and everyone started laughing and carrying on. I was speechless, a condition that rarely happens in my life, and for a long moment I just couldn't make sense of what I was seeing.

"But hold on a minute," I said to David. "I just talked to you in Nashville."

He smiled. "You always figure everything out beforehand," he replied. "This time I wanted to make sure you'd be surprised."

With that, he escorted me into the back of the limo and, getting down on one knee, asked the question I'd been waiting so long to answer with a resounding "Yes!"

The whole night was one of the sweetest, tenderest, and most bothersome in my life. I mean, imagine trying to pull one over on me, the queen of the practical joke? But he did, and I had no choice but to forgive him. As we rode around in the limo through the starry Colorado night I admired the beautiful engagement ring on my finger and called everyone I knew from the car phone.

That car phone, it turned out, was an unexpected bonus to David's elaborate plan. It seems that when he hired the limo company, he'd asked for a bunch of balloons that said "I Love You," which he would release out the moon roof. When the car arrived, however, the balloons read "Happy Anniversary" instead, so the limo company gave him an hour's free calling to make up for the mistake. When I think about it now, those balloons would've come in very handy for all the anniversaries I know we're going to share for the rest of our lives.

So what else could a girl ask for: diplomas from Ding Dong Campus and Redneck Tech; Boss Hogg for a group of loyal backup singers, and a fiancé who's maybe even smarter than I am.

A little humility, maybe? I'll get around to that, but

for right now I'm just enjoying the wonderful journey of my life. Like I said, there are no accidents. Meeting David, being a part of Point Of Grace—it's all happened for a reason. And if we can have a couple of laughs along the way, I guess that proves that God's got a sense of humor, too. I mean, He made me, didn't He?

SHELLEY PHILLIPS

Shelley Lynn Phillips, 2 years old.

Me at 3, looking like a
perfect little angel.

Queen of the World
at age 5.

Dyeing Easter
eggs in 1975.
(I should have
been a chemist.)

My parents and me in 1976.

Me, 12, and Robyn, 4,
on Easter, 1981.

Me and my
sister, Robyn,
on vacation
in Florida, 1981.

Miss America, 1991—er,
make that first runner-up,
Miss O.B.U.

Hanging with my sis
at Christmas, 1993.

The Point Of Grace mothers at the Dove Awards, April 1994.
(Left to right: my mom, Sharon; Denise's mom, Janice; Terry's
mom, Bonnie; and Heather's mom, Brenda.)

For Our Young Fans

Whether we like it or not, being a singing group like Point Of Grace carries with it the responsibility of being role models. It's more than a little intimidating, some nights, to stand in front of a crowded auditorium and realize that we're looked at not just to entertain but also to set an example. Everything we do, good, bad, or indifferent, has the potential of being a justification for someone else doing the same thing. It's not a responsibility we asked for, but it's not one we can ignore either.

That's especially true when a lot of the faces we see looking back at us belong to young people. Our teenage years may be behind us now, but that doesn't mean we've forgotten the feelings, the fears, and the fragile hopes of that difficult time.

When kids come to us for advice and direction, it's not hard to see that the issues they deal with today are even more challenging and critically important than the ones we faced growing up. Sex, drugs, lifestyle choices . . . they can all become life-and-death decisions. No wonder it sometimes seems that adults just don't understand, that when they look at kids all they see is a problem that has to be solved. Don't they understand how hard it is just growing up?

Well, maybe they do, but when you're a teen it's easy to confuse concern for coddling or knowledge for nagging. You've got to find out everything for yourself, even if that means making mistakes that aren't so easy to correct.

The reality is it has never been more important for kids to know what they believe and have the courage to stand by their convictions, no matter how uncool it might be. By hopefully providing a little perspective, a few practical answers to pressing questions, as well as just some simple encouragement and empathy, we're doing what we can to live up to your expectations. The rest is up to you.

Q: Am I too young to date?

Denise: That depends on the person asking. Some are ready at sixteen and some aren't ready at twenty-five. My parents wouldn't let me car-date until I was sixteen, and I'm really glad they made that rule. You know, when you're ten or twelve or fourteen there's so much going on in your life, so many changes. Guys are bouncing off the walls with their hormones and they don't really have a clue about what's happening inside. Neither do girls.

I think you can go out with groups of friends and have a lot of fun. Growing up, I did that all the time with church and school groups. You can have a better time with more people, and it doesn't all have to be so serious.

What are a guy and a girl going to do by themselves at thirteen? If you're going out together alone, you might think you have to kiss him and make out. That's a big deal and a lot of pressure and I think the least amount of pressure you put on yourself, the better off you are.

Heather: Groups are a blast. You can go bowling. I mean how boring is it with two people when you can go bowling with ten? It's just so much more fun. And it's safe that way; you're accountable to everybody who you're with. Also, I think it's so important to be friends before you start dating someone. Make sure that you share common interests.

Terry: Everybody has different maturity levels. My first date was when I was thirteen. It was a foursome and my date's mom drove us in a van. We went to see a movie, and right afterward, she brought us back home. It wasn't like an eighteen-year-old guy coming to pick me up and go parking. You just have to be wise about it and keep yourself out of the dark.

I think a lot of times parents fail to set boundaries. They just don't think about those things, and they let their daughters go out on dates when they're too young. They're setting their kids up for a big fall.

Shelley: I would say to parents, set rules that are firm without feeling like you're the worst mom or dad in the world or that your kid is absolutely deprived because they can't go on a car date. I would say exercise your authority as a parent. If I have a daughter, I think I'll wait until she's at least sixteen before I let her date. People might think that's old-fashioned, but that's just the problem. Everything happens too quickly these days!

Q: Do I owe him a kiss after a nice night out?

Terry: You don't have to kiss anybody if you don't want to. Some guys think: "Hey, I paid for your dinner. Now, what are you going to do for me?" If you don't like him, you don't owe him anything. Now, on the other hand, if you do like him, I don't think there's anything wrong with a kiss.

I don't think I ever kissed on a first date, but it was because I didn't know the person well enough. I like to really get to know someone before I commit to a kiss. And kissing to me is a commitment. It's saying, "I really like you." If you don't like them, then you're giving them the wrong idea.

Remember, you can just stand at the door and say, "Well, thank you so much," and walk in. Relax. Be smart. It's common sense.

Of course, I have friends who go on first dates and make out. And they don't think it's wrong . . . they're fine with it. You have to decide for yourself. None of us are the voice of anyone else's conscience.

Shelley: If a guy takes you out on a nice date and is respectful to you, you owe him the same thing back.

You owe it to him to be a good conversationalist, to be nice and polite and grateful. That's all.

Denise: You don't owe anybody anything. If they ask you out and they pay for it because they like you, then let them pay for it. That's their choice. We need to care about ourselves enough to know that we have ownership of our own bodies. If you had a great time and you like the person and you want to give him a kiss, well fine . . . but you sure don't have to.

Heather: I can honestly say that I did kiss on a first date, but it was just a peck, no big deal. What I enjoy is the anticipation. Like the last guy I dated didn't kiss me on the first date, and it kind of left me wondering, "When is it going to happen?" That's kind of exciting. You have something to look forward to.

It was actually a couple of dates later that we kissed. And I was the one who did it because I thought that he was shy. I kissed him and he said, "Well, I don't normally kiss this early in a relationship." And I thought, "Oh Lord! He thinks I'm so aggressive and I'm really not." So it works both ways.

Q: Should I do a lot of dating or go steady?

Denise: I dated one guy all through high school and into college and I wouldn't trade that in for the world. Looking back now, I needed him as a friend as I went through my ups and downs, and he was consistently there for me. Everyone else thought I was just bubbly and happy all the time, but he saw a side of me that only he and my family really knew. He was there. I could cry with him, and he cared for me through the hard times.

But when you're young, you need to have fun. If there's only one guy you care about dating, go for it. If not, there's nothing wrong with dating someone different every weekend. Now, I think you need to be careful about how many of those people you're kissing. If you're casually dating, then just be sure to keep it casual.

Heather: Some people meet in school and end up getting married. But it's hard for me to comprehend something like that because I had so many friends who had steady dates in high school and then when they got to college they broke up. You get to college and you're dating all these different people and it's great fun. So I guess it depends on the person and what they're looking for.

Shelley: My sister is a freshman in college and she's been dating the same guy for about two years now. But that is so not me! Maybe I just never met anybody who I wanted to be with on a regular basis when I was in high school. I definitely don't think you should limit yourself because you feel insecure, that is, you feel you have to have a boyfriend. Be happy with the person you are; you can't count on somebody else to make you complete. If I don't have a boyfriend, I know I can find other things to occupy my time. Maybe it won't be as much fun alone, but you shouldn't settle for second best just because you're scared of being by yourself.

Terry: While I didn't date a lot in high school, I was more active socially in college. It was great just to go out with a lot of different guys because I could discover the sort of person I liked being with. I learned from every relationship I had. Dating was a valuable experience because being with other guys made me realize how important Chris was to me.

On the other hand, some people, like Heather's parents, are fine just dating one person. They met in grade school and then they married and have been together for thirty years. I'm not sure that would have worked for me.

Q: What message am I sending with my choice of clothes and makeup?

Shelley: You know, we've had so many dads and moms come up to us and say, "Thank you so much for the way you dress. We really appreciate it, because our daughters want to dress like you. And you never wear anything low cut, too short, or too tight." Let me tell you, sometimes that's really hard to do with the way fashion is now. We were so ticked off when last season's clothes came out, because everything was so tight. It was all these little dresses with only one button buttoned.

We're just like anyone else . . . we want to dress cool. I'm a twenty-six-year-old woman and I like clothes! Sometimes, when I'm flipping through a fashion magazine, there's just nothing I'd let myself be seen in. I think girls need to realize that we don't get turned on the same way guys do. If I see a guy without a shirt at the gym, I might say, "Well, he's got a good-looking body or he works out a lot," but it doesn't make me want to have sex with him. But guys are different. They see a girl with a tight shirt or a thin bra and they're turned on physically.

I think some girls are just oblivious when it comes to the effect they're having on guys. Hey, if you don't want your boyfriend to take advantage of you, then don't wear stuff that will provoke him! Dress like you want to be treated.

Heather: When you wear something sexy, if it's too short or too tight or reveals too much skin, you're sending off a message that says, "Maybe I'm that kind of girl."

It's the same way with makeup. Ever since I was little I've loved makeup, but I wasn't allowed to wear it until I was in junior high. My mom would say, "Don't grow up too fast. Be a little girl for a while longer!" And now I look at little girls and say the same thing. A lot of them are trying really hard to be so old. They're thirteen, going on eighteen!

Denise: Some girls at age fourteen naturally look twenty. They have these perfect bodies. I never looked like that when I was twelve or thirteen. I was flat as a pancake!

But sometimes young girls start developing, and because they do, they're going to look older and they have to be careful about the way they dress so that they don't send out a signal that says "I want you to look at my body." You can look cute and dress really hip without having a skirt up to your thigh or having your cleavage show everything. It's all in the way you come across.

Terry: The very first summer that we toured as Point Of Grace, we had these outfits with stretch pants and little jackets and someone came up to us afterward and said, "I know what you're doing is right, and I believe in your message, but your outfits really kept us from listening to you."

And that's true. I know when I watch people onstage, if they're wearing something that's attracting my attention more than what they're saying, that's what I'm going to focus on. So, it's especially important for us to dress appropriately. I mean, if we dress like Madonna and act like a Christian, where is the consistency in that? You just have to be very aware.

Q: Some of my friends drink and do drugs. Are they still my friends?

Denise: Of course they're still your friends. Maybe you've grown up with them before your paths went in different ways, but they're still your friends. I knew people in high school who drank and partied. They knew that I didn't do that stuff and so they didn't do it around me. In that way I hope maybe I was a positive influence. I took them to church with me whenever I could and I was glad that they accepted me, knowing the beliefs that I had. You've got to ask yourself, "How can I make an impact on someone if I'm not even going to be their friend?"

Terry: It's important that they know you care. They know that drugs and alcohol aren't good for them. They hear it every day, so maybe they don't need to hear it from you, too. But they do need to know that you're concerned, that you don't want them to ruin their lives.

Of course, there's a risk in letting people know what you really think. They may say "Forget you!" and turn it around to make it seem like you're judging them. But if you'll still continue to love them, there's at least a chance they'll change.

When some disaster happens in their life, most of the time those people end up turning back to somebody who was honest enough to say, "I care about you and I'm worried about you."

Then there are those people who are so extreme in their behavior that it's better just to stay away. But, generally, if you're strong enough in your beliefs and you know who you are, then you can handle being their friend because you won't be going out partying with them just to prove something.

Shelley: I had a really good girlfriend in high school who always came back to me in the hard times. She starting drinking and doing drugs, but she'd always come back to talk to me when things got rough. I think she knew she was playing with fire, but she needed someone to tell her what she couldn't admit to herself. I was a friend who was at least a little grounded.

Q: Why can't I see the same movies and TV as my friends?

Terry: What you put into your head is going to show itself in what you do and how you act. A lot of what you see on TV today—especially MTV—is appalling. They're telling kids, "This is the 1990s, this is pop culture, and this is cool." That's just a lie! You have to be very careful about what you see and hear, because it's going to affect the way you live your life.

Denise: I think you have to be very particular about R-rated movies. Find out why it has got that rating—for sex, or violence, or language, or all three. That's why those ratings are there. When you're young and impressionable, you need to follow the rules for your own good.

But at the same time, it's not always so easy to make that decision. In our case, we have to be very careful. We may see a movie that we feel is all right for us, but not for some of our fans. And if they hear that we've been to see it, they may say, "Oh, well, if they saw it, I guess it's okay for me, too." That's a big responsibility to carry.

Shelley: I wish I could say I was the most disciplined person in the world and that I don't go to see those movies, but sometimes I do. It depends on the subject matter. Is it all about sex? Because to me that's different from just an action adventure movie with a lot of fake violence.

If we remove ourselves from the culture and what's

going on around us, then how in the world are we going to relate to people who are in that culture?

Heather: It's a question of personal conviction. Some people, like the Christian singer Carmen, have said, "God told me I shouldn't go to any R-rated movies," and he never does. That's something God has really spoken to him about, and if it comes to a point in my life where God says, "You know what? This is not glorifying me. Here's where I want you to draw a line," then that's what I'll do, although it's never easy. Until that time, I've got to make decisions based on what my conscience tells me.

Q: How can I best help a friend in trouble?

Denise: When we volunteered as counselors at the Crisis Pregnancy Center, we learned right away not to pretend that we had all the answers.

But what you can do is just be there for somebody. Call them and say, "Hey, I'm thinking about you today," or just sit quietly while they cry. You might have to admit that "I may not know how to help you, but I'll be here and I'll listen to you."

Terry: People just want you to listen sometimes. If you think you've got a solution to everything, you're really putting yourself in a dangerous position. Get to know somebody and to love them before barging into their lives and saying, "Here's what you need to do to change!" You're just going to offend them. I know I'd be offended by that attitude.

As Christians we have to be careful, when we share what we believe, that we're not just reading off a bunch of rules. If you come on too strong, that's what turns people away from God. They're going to end up worse off than when they first met you.

Heather: How you conduct yourself around people makes a big difference. If you're judgmental and unforgiving, they're going to be less likely to come to you when they have a problem. If you're always pointing out their faults and sins, they're going to be afraid to share with you for fear of what you might say.

But if you let them know that you're going to love them and be honest with them no matter what, it's going to make all the difference.

Q: Is it wrong to betray a confidence, no matter what?

Heather: I remember once when I was in college a friend of mine picked me up for a date, and he had drugs in his car.

This was a person I had known for a long time, and I felt that this could really ruin his life, not to mention getting me in a lot of hot water. I wasn't sure what to do: should I keep this in confidence, or should I tell somebody?

Well, I ended up telling someone else and that person confronted my friend and today he's not doing drugs, so it all worked out all right. But it wasn't an easy decision to make.

Shelley: It depends on the problem. If the secret is something really life threatening, like wanting to commit suicide, you've got a responsibility to find help, no matter what.

Sometimes I think maybe people tell you things in confidence because they really want you to help them. They're crying out for help.

Terry: If it really is a secret that they don't want shared, then it's risky to betray that confidence. It may make the whole situation worse. In any case, you should probably pray hard and really seek God's guidance. Without naming the person or situation, you could even hint around for guidance from other people.

Q: Sometimes I feel so shy and awkward. Why?

Terry: Join the club. We all feel that way at one time or another. But you can't really make too many changes on the outside, unless you want to pay big bucks for plastic surgery, and that's a waste of money in the end anyway. All you can really change is what's on the inside. In the Bible, in Proverbs, there's a list of things that God wants a woman to be, and I've looked at that a lot of times and said, "God, I can't do this!" But He wants me to try. Doing that, striving to be beautiful on the inside, helps solve the problem of looking so much at one's outward appearance.

Denise: Everyone feels self-conscious about themselves at one time or another. And there's such an awkward stage you go through when you're a teenager. Let me tell you, I was ugly! I look at pictures of myself back then and I get so embarrassed! I had buck teeth and had to get braces to fix them.

Heather: You can still have pimples when you're twenty-five. They don't just go away when you grow up. You just have to learn to deal with it. I suggest getting some makeup and do a little more spot removal.

Kids need to know all of us have gone through ugly stages. I'm sure Julia Roberts probably had her gawky period. Well, maybe not her, but you get the basic idea.

Shelley: We all have our serious ugly days—when we wake up and realize, "Okay, today's not going to be my day." So you just wear a hat or something. I remember in high school, looking at those girls who seemed like every day they're perfect. And I'm sure that even they felt ugly once or twice.

But kids just need to know that when they're going through that awkward stage, part of it is that they just haven't figured out how to make the most of what they've got. I can see a progression in myself in family photos from when I was a kid to when my mom let me wear a little lip gloss to when I figured out a better hairstyle and then maybe got to wear a little makeup. It's all part of a process, and you have to realize that five or ten years later the end result is going to be different from what it is today. Hang in there.

Q: Are my parents always right?

Terry: Nobody's always right. If you don't agree with

them, I think it's okay to ask why, but remember, we're supposed to honor and obey our parents.

That might be hard for kids who don't have parents who are very honorable. It's easy for us to say to them, "Respect your parents." Most of the time our parents made good decisions. But when your mom or dad makes wrong decisions, well, that's when you have to look to God to find the right answer.

We also have to learn to make our own decisions. I remember when I was choosing what college I wanted to go to, my mom and dad gave me their input and told me what they thought, but they never really said "yes" or "no."

Shelley: There's also something to be said for obeying your parents when you don't think they're right. They're not setting up rules because they don't like you or they want to make your lives dull and boring. They set up rules to protect you.

Heather: I remember bringing home kids from school who my parents weren't that crazy about, and looking back now I think, "You know what? They were right." I think parents have a sixth sense.

Denise: Sadly, there are a lot of kids whose parents just don't care. Or, worse, might direct them the wrong way. I don't know what to say about those situations. I hate to tell them "You should do exactly what your parents say" when it's obvious that the parents themselves are out of control. Maybe the best thing is to go to your pastor or your youth minister and get their advice.

Q: Do my parents really understand the pressure I'm under?

Heather: I think they understand more than we give them credit for. They've been there, and while some of the things we go through today are probably different from what they went through, a lot of them are the same. I mean, there's nothing new about drinking and making out.

Looking back on my own life, I wish I would have let my parents in on a little more about what was happening with me. There were times when I let my guard down and told them things I'd done that I wasn't very proud of. They always surprised me with how understanding they were. If you don't let your parents in on anything, how can you expect them to make a decision or give you advice without knowledge of the situation?

Shelley: It's all about learning how to deal with authority. Ultimately things are going to work out a lot better for you if you obey those in authority in your life. If you're butting heads with them about every single thing, you're going to be miserable and you're not going to have a very easy time in life. By following the rules you can avoid a lot of problems, and things will be smoother all around.

Terry: I can remember times when I wanted to spend the night at someone's house and my parents said, "No, you're staying home tonight." I'd really pitch a fit! It all seemed so horribly unfair, and I made it worse for myself because I sat there and sulked instead of enjoying the time with my family. What I wouldn't give just to be able to be with them right now!

As kids, the things we think are so important are really pretty trivial. Once we become adults, we've got bigger problems to deal with. But I guess you just have to experience that for yourself.

Q: Can parents be too strict?

Denise: Yes. There's a fine line between sheltering your child and smothering them. It's a parent's job to teach their kids about reality. When they leave home, they're going to face a lot of challenges and problems, and they have to be ready to handle that. I'm not a parent yet and I realize that it's a tough job. You don't want your child to be naive about the world around them, but they don't necessarily have to experience every bit of it either.

Heather: If you think your parents are being too strict, you should talk to them about how you feel, as long as you do it in a controlled manner, not yelling and screaming. Unfortunately, there are situations where parents are so strict and unbending they don't even hear what their kids are trying to say.

Shelley: I remember when I was growing up, if my mom or dad told me I couldn't do something, I was allowed to say, "Well I don't agree, and I want you to tell me why." They understood that being told "no" sometimes made me mad and that my emotions needed to be expressed. Some parents run their homes like boot camp. There's no talking back, no questioning a decision.

I would encourage parents not to just say "No, because I said so." Maybe your kids will do what you say when they're younger, but when they get older, they're going to start asking questions and wanting to know why.

You can say, "I don't want you to watch that TV show because I said so." Well why? And maybe if you said, "Because your mother and I want to honor Christ in our house, right down to the TV programs that we watch." Now, what's a kid going to say to that? But a parent better be careful what they watch on TV, too. Practice what you preach!

Terry: Respectfully asking your parents why they made a certain decision might cause them to think more about what they decide. Then you might respond better to that "no" when you understand the reason.

But, of course, if your parents are upset, then maybe it's better to approach them when the issue isn't so sensitive, when you can sit down with them and say, "Two weeks ago you said I couldn't do this. Could you tell me why?" That's hard to do, but it might help clear things up between you.

Q: Sometimes my brothers and sisters really get to me. What should I do?

Heather: Usually if you just punch them and knock them out it keeps them quiet for a while!

Seriously, you're going to have fights with your brothers and sisters. That's healthy as long as it's under control. That's how you learn to get along with people in the real world. The four of us try to work together, and if it weren't for having to build those relationships with our sisters, learning to share things and make allowances, we wouldn't get along nearly as well as we do.

Shelley: I fought a lot with my sister when she was younger. She always wanted to be with me. I can honestly say now that I wish I had included her, but I didn't want to be around her because it wasn't cool. I regret that, because she really thought I just hated her for a while. I was so insensitive.

But you know what? Your brothers and sister are also the ones who will stand up for you when others don't. They'll be there for you long after your school friends are gone. I now know my sister will be there for me, and I'll be there for her, in any situation.

Denise: I've learned that most of the time when you fight, it's because you're being selfish, wanting your own way. Learning to give to others is hard to do, but it's something that you can learn.

My older sister taught me a lot. She was always the angel, and when my middle sister and I fought she would tell us we needed to say we're sorry. I never wanted to hear that, but it was true. We had to learn to say we were wrong once in a while.

Terry: I remember my sisters and I used to fight about clothes. All four of us wore each other's outfits and my mom's, too. And we had battles over the little bathroom we had to share. That was a big deal, too, disrespecting each other's hair spray and shampoo.

But there's a special bond you have with your sisters that you don't have with anybody else. You can go two months without talking to them and call them up and then share your heart and understand each other perfectly, more than you would with a friend.

Q: What can I do to strengthen family bonds?

Shelley: Sometimes you need to take the initiative. Spend time hanging out with your family instead of just your friends. Don't make your parents always have to insist on family time. Because sometimes they won't, if they think you don't want anything to do with them. Maybe they would love for you to be around, but they just don't want to ask. Let them know you enjoy being part of the family.

When I was growing up, we always ate dinner together. That was our treasured time, when we could all talk about what had happened to us that day, and catch up with each other. And later, when I was in college and met friends who never had that special connection, I realized how really lucky I was.

Denise: I think that you can take a lot of stress off of your parents by helping out around the house or just trying to make life a little easier for others. It seems kids that come from divorced families tend to be better about that. The ones who grew up in single-parent homes learned how to help out a lot sooner than we did.

Kids need to know that parents have feelings. I remember sometimes hurting my mom's feelings, without even thinking about it. I could have been more sensitive. We don't see them behind the doors, crying. We need to be sensitive to know that parents are real people, and that we can wound them.

Q: How important is a college education?

Terry: I think you grow up a lot in college. It concerns me sometimes when kids get married right out of high school because they haven't experienced a lot of life yet. Juggling jobs and a marriage is a lot for a couple to take on at a young age. But that doesn't mean you can't make it work either.

Heather: A lot of kids can't afford to go to college, and they need to know it's not the be-all and end-all. Not going to college doesn't mean you can't be a success. You can still provide for yourself and be an effective member of society.

Denise: It's important to learn and to keep learning, no matter how you go about it. It's good to expand your mind—not that I remember one single thing I learned in college!

You can only learn so much from books. Relationships and personal growth are things I found out about once I got out of the house and into college. It was hard for me to go off by myself, but that's when I learned what it meant to be independent.

AFTERWORD

Well, it has truly been an incredible experience writing this book for you. We've learned so much about ourselves along the way. Hopefully, you've also gotten to know us a little better.

As individuals, of course, we continue to change and be challenged daily, trying our best to deepen our relationship with Christ and be responsible with all He's given us. And as a group, we've had our share of successes and hard times, but the good far outweighs the bad. We're so honored to have had a gold-selling album and eleven number-one singles, but by far the best part has been traveling and meeting you. Really, the credit for what has happened to us belongs to you. You've supported us, encouraged us, and prayed for us. We've worked hard to make "POG" a reality, and we'll keep at it for as long as you'll let us.

In the meantime, we hope this book, like our music, will help you find your own way through some of the mysteries of life and love. Our experiences, the history we have in common, and the convictions that give our lives purpose are things we've been privileged to share with all of you. If any of it has been a help, we hope you'll pass it along, because if there's one thing we've learned through all the crazy twists and turns our lives have taken together, it's that the best way to receive God's love is to give it away.

Thanks for letting us share with you the wonders of His love.